101
THERAPEUTIC
SUCCESSES

Overcoming Transference
and Resistance in Psychotherapy

Gerald Schoenewolf, Ph.D.

JASON ARONSON INC.
Northvale, New Jersey
London

For Jane, with gratitude

Library of Congress Cataloging-in-Publication Data

Schoenewolf, Gerald.
  101 therapeutic successes.

  1. Psychotherapy–Case studies. I. Title.
II. Title: One hundred one therapeutic successes.
RC465.S36 1989   616.89'14   88–7612
ISBN 0-87668-869-5

Manufactured in the United States of America. Jason Aronson Inc. offers books and cassettes. For information and catalog write to Jason Aronson Inc., 230 Livingston Street, Northvale, New Jersey 07647.

Contents

PART TWO: INTERVENTIONS OF THE MIDDLE PHASE

Preface

What is a therapeutic success and how is it achieved? This book is intended to provide a detailed, organized review of the range of successful therapeutic interventions. In my previous book, *101 Common Therapeutic Blunders* (co-authored with Richard C. Robertiello, M.D.), I focused on the errors that occur when therapists have not successfully analyzed either the patient's transference and resistance or their own countertransference and counterresistance. In the present volume, which serves as a sequel to the previous one, I concentrate on the successful interventions that result from cases in which therapists *have* analyzed transference and resistance—both their own and that of their patients.

101 Therapeutic Successes is divided into three sections: Interventions of the Beginning Phase, Interventions of the Middle Phase, and Interventions of the Termination Phase. As in the previous volume, this book uses brief vignettes to demonstrate the types of interventions that befit each phase. The vignettes explore the range of interventions at the disposal of therapists, explaining which interventions work best with specific character types, when they should be employed, and why they are successful. In addition, I have attempted to create vivid portraits of both patients and therapists so that the reader can understand them not just as clinical entities but as human beings.

Like its predecessor, this book is aimed at those in all branches of the helping professions as well as those lay people interested in how therapy works.

The case histories in this book, while based on actual cases, have been modified to preserve anonymity and to illustrate points more dramatically. Most were based on the author's clinical experience or on the work of colleagues. A few were suggested by ideas from the writings of Frieda Fromm-Reichmann, Ralph Greenson, Jay Haley, Jacob Kirman, Heinrich Racker, Hyman Spotnitz, and D. W. Winnicott.

I would like to express my appreciation to Richard G. Robertiello, M.D., and Jason Aronson, M.D., for their help in formulating this book.

Introduction

The Nature of Therapeutic Success

About Therapeutic Success

One seldom hears therapists use the word "cure." The term has fortunately gone out of favor. People do not generally want to think of themselves as sick and in need of being cured. Nor should they. Freud observed that it takes a person with a fairly healthy ego to lie on a couch and take an objective look at himself. Confucius expressed much the same sentiment more than 3,000 years ago, lamenting that he had traveled far and wide and had not found a single man who could "bring home the judgment against himself." Sages throughout history have viewed the capacity for self-study as a sine qua non of mental health. To use the term "cure" with respect to the process of therapy, whatever the kind, is to put a negative framework on it; those who seek therapy and stick to it are generally more open to exploring themselves. They do not seek a "cure" from sickness so much as an affirmation of their healthy inclinations. They seek somebody who will help them become more truly themselves.

Not that people come to therapy in order to gain enlightenment; they do not. For the most part, they come to relieve their pain. They cannot relate to family values that have been destructive to them. They cannot relate to cultural entities–whether they be large corporations or small clubs, large political movements or small religious institutions–that extend these destructive values into society through ideological or religious belief systems. They cannot adjust even to healthy systems, for their responses have become inappropriate to the situations that face them. They are out of harmony with themselves and with others. Yet there remains locked inside of them a small kernel of life that is repulsed by the falsity of their existence, which offers them only secondary, narcissistic, or neurotic gratifications. There is within them a longing for intimacy, without which life has little meaning. So, although people do not come to therapy saying, "I want to find the truth" or "I want genuine intimacy," that is in fact why they are there.

Even people suffering from the more severe forms of narcissism–such as schizophrenics–loathe being categorized as "sick" and in need of a "cure," as R. D. Laing pointed out. Some professionals use labels to stigmatize people and keep them entrapped in their state of withdrawal, thereby gratifying some narcissistic need of their own. When individuals are labeled, they often respond to this symbolic suggestion by playing the roles assigned to them. Indeed, therapists may unwittingly perpetuate the same destructive relationships that the patients experienced in their families. Terms for classifying and understanding human beings according to their deviations from healthy functioning are certainly necessary; however, such terms are best utilized mainly for erecting theories and conducting research, and not for work in the clinic or office. Some terms are unavoidable even in the clinic, such as the word "patient." Of course, there are other words–analysand, client, and so on–but none is exactly right for all who seek the help of a therapist. So "patient" is still in use, but the concept of "cure" has been discarded.

There is another reason why the word "cure" is seldom used today. During the years since psychoanalysis and psychotherapy were invented, the length of time the average person spends in therapy has grown longer. One-year analyses have given way to multi-year therapy and psychoanalytic cases. There are two main reasons for this. As our knowledge of the therapy procedure has expanded, we have discovered that there is more to it than Freud and the other pioneers initially thought. Whereas in Freud's day therapists focused mainly on resolving the Oedipus, castration, or masculinity complexes, now we are more likely to emphasize earlier fixations. In addition, while Freud's patients were primarily neurotics of the obsessive or hysterical variety, today's patients are more likely to be narcissistic, borderline, and sometimes even psychotic. Whether this means our society is growing less healthy is an arguable point. Whatever the case, more and more of today's psychoanalysts and therapists agree that there is no such thing as a "cure"; the most we can do is restore some measure of spontaneity by slowly chipping away at an individual's grandiosity, by slowly releasing the rage, and by gradually modeling a new, more healthy way of relating. We strive to help the individual work through resistance, undo repression, and regain a capacity for trust that will enable a revival of the essentials of effective bonding.

Freud grappled with the issue of therapeutic "cure" in his paper, "Analysis Terminable and Interminable." He seemed to resign himself to the limitations of the process, with respect to the types of personalities that seemed at the time amenable to psychoanalysis, and in terms of how much of a transformation of character was possible, even with increasingly lengthy analyses. Other psychoanalysts have since echoed this view. Freud asserted that the two strongest transference resistances that therapists had to deal with—the ones most instrumental in defeating therapy—were penis envy in females (which took the form of a refusal to "submit" to a male therapist's suggestions), and castration fear in the male (which took the form of a struggle against "his passive or feminine attitude" toward another male). There would also be, following Freud's thinking, a corresponding resistance by female patients to female therapists (in this case taking the form of a struggle against homosexual feelings and the fear of re-engulfment by Mother). Because of these deep-seated resistances, complete cures were not possible.

In this paper Freud does not use the word "cure" but speaks instead of success. The factors that he felt were decisive for therapeutic success were threefold: undoing the effects of traumatic etiology, controlling the instincts, and altering the ego. As the result of traumatic experiences, the ego develops various defense mechanisms designed for avoiding danger, anxiety, and unpleasure. However, in psychoanalysis the defense mechanisms directed to a former danger recur in the treatment procedure as resistances against recovery. The task of the analyst is to make conscious to the ego what is repressed in the id and to modify the defense mechanisms to meet present situations in a more appropriate fashion. If this task is achieved, the therapy can be said to be successful.

In his final paper on the therapy procedure, "Constructions in Analysis" (published in 1937), Freud clarified the aims of the analytic process. The work of analysis aims at inducing the patient to "give up repressions belonging to his early development and to replace them by reactions of a sort that would correspond to a psychically mature condition." The patient had to be brought to recollect traumatic experiences and the "affective impulses called up by them." His present symptoms and inhibitions were the consequences, Freud believed, of repressions of such memories and feelings. He compared the work of analysis to that of an archeologist's excavation.

About the Various Methods of Psychotherapy

Like Freud, Sandor Ferenczi was concerned about the ever-lengthening analyses. He was the first to experiment with what he called "active therapy techniques." Many followed his path—most notably Wilhelm Reich. They spawned a plethora of

modern therapy techniques from Gestalt therapy to bioenergetics to Rolphing. Ferenczi was also the first to emphasize that the
success of a therapy depends largely on the degree of the therapist's countertransference.

Things have not changed all that much since the early days
of psychoanalysis with respect to the nature of therapeutic
success. We still have those who practice more or less classical
analysis, and we also have those who practice some form of active
therapy. Whatever the technique, the aim is generally the same,
though couched in different terminology. Today's therapist
might speak of getting the patient in touch with his feelings
rather than of making conscious the unconscious, but the
meaning is similar. However, the debate still continues between
psychoanalytic and active psychotherapists as to which method
works better. There are also debates between schools of psychoanalysis and between schools of active therapy.

Hypnotherapists who follow the procedures of Milton
Erickson claim they can evade the analysis of transference and
resistance entirely by communicating directly with the patient's
unconscious through hypnosis. They also claim their "cures"
represent more than just the removal of symptoms and that they
are permanent. This contradicts the experiences of Freud and
other psychoanalysts who abandoned hypnosis in favor of free
association. They contend that hypnosis is a transference cure,
and therefore can only be temporary in nature. Cathartic thera-
pies such as psychodrama, bioenergetics, and primal therapy
disavow the analysis of transference and resistance while
stressing the reliving of traumas. Gestalt, which emphasizes
here-and-now experimentation, does not give much importance
to the reconstruction of early childhood events. Psychoanalysts
counter that without the analysis of transference and resistance,
particularly as it occurs between the patient and the therapist,
patients will not learn firsthand how they overdefend and defeat
themselves; catharsis and getting in touch with present feelings
are only part of the process of change, and not the whole process.

Among psychoanalysts, self psychologists argue that interpretation is seldom necessary, whereas classical analysts counter that interpretation is the most vital intervention. Ego psychologists emphasize the analysis of the ego, id, and superego; object relationists stress the relationship between the self and external objects; while modern psychoanalysts encourage the development of the negative transference, sometimes by actively provoking it.

As research on the viability of the various methods of psychotheraphy has accumulated, it has shown that there is no one method that is right for all patients all of the time, and that the crucial element in any method is the rapport between patient and therapist. Whatever the method, the patient must feel cared about. For this reason, many therapists have developed an eclectic methodology, borrowing from a number of methods, depending on the type of patient they are treating and where that patient is in terms of development. Each patient determines his or her own interventions.

During the course of my own practice I have tried both active and analytic techniques and have found a place for a range of interventions, depending on the nature of the therapeutic task at hand. In my groups I use Gestalt, bioenergetics, art therapy, and other active techniques. In individual sessions I have found that hypnotic techniques can be useful in working with certain personality types, such as phobic patients or those with multiple personalities. However, when I use such a parameter, I explain to the patient that we are deviating from standard technique solely to pursue a particular aim, as is advised by the Blancks in their book *Ego Psychology*. Once that aim has been achieved, we return to standard procedure. Standard procedure consists of psychoanalytic therapy – use of the couch, therapeutic neutrality, free association, dream interpretation, the analysis of transference and resistance, and historical reconstruction. Mostly I see a patient once a week, sometimes twice a week, rarely more often. Frequency of sessions does not seem to have any impact on how long a case takes to evolve; therefore I do not particularly encourage more frequent sessions. In general I use a modern psychoanalytic style, looking for and encouraging the development as soon as possible of the patient's negative transference (feelings of anger, jealousy, revenge, and the like). This is done because many narcissistic patients tend to act out these feelings by leaving therapy if they are not encouraged to verbalize them to the therapist.

In the view of modern psychoanalysts, the leading cause of mental illness – and of human misery – is repressed aggression. To be human is to be aggressive. If that aggression is dealt with in socially constructive ways, the door is then open to effective bonding with significant others. But when aggression is thwarted by an environment that does not allow for the maturational needs of the individual, the aggression gets repressed by the individual. Repressed individuals separate themselves from others, acting out aggression in indirect, hostile, and destructive ways. Until the negative transference is drawn out and analyzed, the patient will not develop a truly positive transference, a good working alliance, and a receptivity to the therapist's interpretations.

Whether or not it is possible to achieve therapeutic success without the analysis of transference and resistance remains a point of contention, one that may be resolved by more conclusive research on therapeutic outcomes. The difficulty with all such research is that it is hard to tell whether an outcome is successful or not, depending on who is doing the assessment and by what criteria the assessment is being made. To be a therapist is to have a bias that one's own cases have been successful, or that one's own school is more successful than another. However, if the aim of therapy is a change in the character of the patient, and not just the removal of symptoms, a lasting change is more likely to come out of a long-term therapeutic relationship in which transference and resistance have been analyzed and resolved.

About Therapeutic Interventions

Each of the cases in this book describes an instance in which a therapeutic intervention led to an advance in therapeutic progress. By "advance" I mean any instance in which the patient's transference and resistance have been addressed and the neurotic or narcissistic defense mechanisms have to some extent been resolved. When that happens, the patient's behavior undergoes some kind of change. At times this change occurs abruptly, following some remark or action by the therapist, and at other times it occurs gradually, during the course of an ongoing intervention. When the patient's response is an abrupt one, it may take various forms, including an "Ah-ha!," an emotional release, or a prolonged period of silence. In other cases, as when a negative transference is resolved, the patient may suddenly stop expressing anger at the therapist and direct it instead at a parent or sibling. When the intervention is ongoing, the change is more gradual and harder to detect. The patient may come on time for sessions when heretofore there had been frequent tardiness, or lie in a more relaxed posture on the couch, or talk more freely about certain subjects. Each therapeutic advance is the result of a successful intervention.

One of the main pitfalls is that of determining whether an intervention has truly been successful. It is well known that there are patients who seem to hear and understand a particular interpretation, only to forget it by the next session. There is the "flight to health" syndrome, in which patients suddenly report feeling better and may even behave in a happy and contented manner for several sessions. In reality they have been frightened by something that came up during the course of therapy, usually some threatening feeling inside of them, most often the feeling of aggression. In general, during the early stages of therapy a patient will try to please the therapist by responding positively to the latter's interventions. Some of the biggest therapeutic errors occur in the beginning phase, since many therapists want to feel potent. Therapists who have not resolved their narcissistic, anal, or oedipal fixations may begin to believe their interventions are really working and then will be in for a shock when the patient suddenly acts out a negative transference. Therefore the best way to determine whether an intervention has really worked is by studying the patient over a period of time.

Therapists use numerous types of interventions. The following are the most common:

Interpreting
Remaining silent and/or still
Listening
Explaining
Instructing
Questioning
Making suggestions
Complimenting
Mirroring
Commanding
Joining the resistance
Challenging the resistance
Identifying with the patient
Giving ultimatums
Threatening or warning a patient
Using paradox or sarcasm
Telling stories or jokes (metaphor or analogy)
Using hypnosis
Using experiential exercises (Gestalt, bioenergetics, primal, etc.)
Giving homework assignments
Expressing feelings to the patient
Sharing self-revelations
Making contracts
Setting deadlines

Hugging and other physical contact (nonsexual)

Early termination (of avoiding, abusive, or out-of-control patients)

Offering telephone sessions

Making house calls

Chastising or lecturing

Making noises (grunts, whistles, etc.) or facial expressions

Prescribing drugs or hospitalization (for psychotics or extremely destructive patients)

Making audio or video recordings of sessions

A successful case is one in which there are numerous successful interventions over a period of years. In the *beginning phase* of treatment—which may last from a few months to several years—the interventions are geared toward educating the patient about the nature of the therapeutic process, handling treatment-destructive resistance (canceling sessions, nonpayment of fees, tardiness, and so on), and establishing a therapeutic alliance. In the *middle phase*—which may last from a few years to many years—the bulk of the working-through is done. The middle phase generally begins when the patient has established a stabilized relationship with the therapist, has formed a rudimentary object transference, and has begun, ever so minimally, to tolerate analysis. During this phase a therapist is more likely to use interpretation, suggestion, experiential exercises, and the like. In the *termination phase*—usually lasting less than a year—the patient is "weaned" from dependence on the therapist and the final working-through is completed. During this phase interpretation may be used exclusively. The kind of intervention one uses is always dependent on the type of patient, on where the patient is, developmentally, and where he or she is going.

Choosing the right intervention at the right time is the art of psychotherapy. In order to do so, the therapist must analyze his own countertransference and counterresistance along with that of his patient. As most therapeutic failures are the result of interventions influenced by countertransference and counter-resistance, most successes result from interventions based on objective analysis of the therapist–patient dyad, a fact emphasized in this book's predecessor, *101 Common Therapeutic Blunders*. Ideally, the therapist uses the feelings that are elicited by patients to better understand them. Those feelings give the therapist a good idea of the kinds of feelings once elicited in the patient by his parents or siblings, and also allow the therapist to judge, experientially, what kind of intervention will be the right one at the moment.

Each of the cases in this book describes a different kind of therapeutic problem, as well as a different kind of personality type. In general, the more severely narcissistic or neurotic patients are, the more difficult they are to work with and the longer it takes to reach a mutually agreed-upon termination. A therapist working with a highly motivated, minimally narcissistic patient who has a fairly healthy ego may achieve therapeutic resolution within a year or so. However, when working with a schizophrenic, it is not unusual for the therapy to require twenty years.

When does a case reach the termination point? Most analysts agree that psychoanalysis is nearing completion when the patient begins to relate to the analyst as a real object, rather than a transference object, self-object, or fetish. Again, there is no such thing as a complete success, and there will always be some transference and some resistance. Other signs of imminent termination relate to how the patient is functioning: Does the patient have healthy relationships? A stable economic situation? Interesting hobbies? Contentment? Emotional stability? Finally, how does the patient deal with aggression? Is he able to handle the aggression of others without undue stress? Has his own aggression been neutralized? After determining that termination is appropriate, there is usually one last bit of work to be done, for generally there is a pretermination regression, brought on by the fear of letting go of the therapist. Termination calls for its own series of interventions.

About Intimacy

In a sense, psychotherapy is a kind of reparenting. Those who come to us usually suffer from the results of faulty parenting. They come locked into patterns of thought, feeling, and behavior that are destructive to themselves and others, looking for a strong figure who will put them right. Our job is to respond to them in a healthy way, in order to correct their self-defeating patterns. Just as a child born with a deformed foot must wear corrective shoes for a few years in order to "mold" his foot in the right way, we serve to correct the maturational "deformities" of our patients. We attempt to reparent them and allow them to blossom as fully mature and actualized adults.

We are teachers of intimacy. Most of our patients have painful memories, often buried under layers of the unconscious, about the intimacy they first experienced in early childhood. They are afraid to trust again and, in fact, often react with anger at anybody who wants their trust or cooperation. When they first come to us, they rail against us, attempt to defeat us, refuse to feel anything for us, try to seduce us, and often set out, unconsciously, to provoke us into behaving as their parents behaved. If we do, they then have confirmation that their way of being and their perspective is right after all (though on some level they doubt it, otherwise they would not have sought therapy). If they fail in this attempt to get us to respond like their parents, we can then teach them how to let go of the unnecessary, inappropriate, and destructive defenses that prevent them from achieving gratifying intimacy with others and with themselves. That is, of course, provided we ourselves have worked through our own blocks to intimacy.

Obviously, to be good teachers of intimacy, we must have achieved intimacy in our own lives. It entails, among other things, being able to accept the full range of feelings directed to us by patients—specifically their aggressive and libidinal feelings—no matter how mean, silly, excessive, or inappropriate they may at first seem. It means having healthy responses to such feelings, responses that encourage intimacy and discourage distancing behavior. It entails allowing full expression verbally while maintaining professional abstinence. Therapists who have not worked through their own blocks tend to hide behind a therapeutic posture—psychoanalytic neutrality, the blank screen, the nurturing therapist (let's not have any negative feelings, please)—using these postures to counterresist certain thoughts or feelings.

Everything that is good about life flows from successful intimate relationships. If an individual has gratifying intimate relationships, he or she will also be a better worker, a better parent, a more productive and contented person. Many have pointed to the importance of a balance between the libidinal and aggressive drives, a fusion that enables people to function smoothly. Invariably when individuals cannot experience intimacy, it has to do with this imbalance. Their ambivalence towards people is great. They cannot allow themselves to be spontaneous. Their aggressive drive overwhelms their libidinal drive; their narcissism precludes the development of object ties; and they seek to control or destroy themselves or others, rather than to relate and be truly themselves.

To be truly ourselves, we must be truly open to another person. It is when we let ourselves and significant others know even those things that we fear will make us most vulnerable—those dark, unthinkable intangibles of the unconscious—and have them accepted, that we experience the greatest joy in living. If we cannot open up to at least one person during our lifetime in this way, we have not really lived at all.

In many cases, we are the first person our patients will open up to in this manner; we are their springboards to intimacy.

PART ONE

INTERVENTIONS OF THE BEGINNING PHASE

Intervention 1

An Initial Interview

"I really don't want to be in therapy for years and years," the young man said. He sat in the chair facing the therapist, his brown eyes guarded, his arms folded. "I just want to work on my problem with auditions. As I told you, I'm an actor, and one of my biggest problems is that every time I do an audition, I get so nervous I blow it. I just want to work on this problem. The rest of my life is okay. I don't want to talk about my childhood and all that stuff. My childhood was fine. I mean, it shouldn't take more than a few months to lick this problem, should it?"

The therapist knew the initial interview was probably the single most important session she would do with this or any patient. It would get things going either on a right or a wrong footing; it would set the framework for the relationship. More than in any other session, her every utterance, gesture, or expression would have a crucial impact. As she listened to the young man, many thoughts occurred to her; yet she said nothing. She understood that the young man was extremely resistant. His fear of wanting to stay in therapy for "years and years" expressed many deeper, as yet unconscious, fears: the fear of dependency, of castration by the Mother-Witch, of his own aggression toward authority figures and of the counteraggression it might elicit, of being seduced by the therapist and then rejected, and of the painful truth of his life and circumstances, especially that truth that would shatter his narcissistic view of himself. She understood that his desire to keep the therapy focused on one problem, avoiding reconstruction and other aspects of therapy, was an attempt to control the process in order to further defend against his fears. She knew all this in an instant and said nothing. In order to calm the young man's fears, she decided to speak only if he asked her to—that is, to feed him only when he wanted to be fed. It was important that he feel as securely in control as he wanted to feel. Not only his fears but the underlying paranoia had to be calmed, in order for a bridge of trust to be formed. He had to be made to feel that the therapist had absolutely no designs on him except to listen to and help him in any way he wished to be helped.

The young man continued to speak for thirty minutes or so, never directly asking the therapist for a comment, although he glanced at her frequently, as if to seek confirmation. Each time he did so, the therapist nodded, and sometimes smiled. Finally he stopped, looked at the therapist at length, and asked, "So what do you think? Do you think you can help me?"

"Sure," she replied without hesitation, smiling cordially.

"But I don't want it to take years and years."

"I understand."

"I just want to work on the problem I have with auditions. How long do you think it will take?"

"I can't tell you that," she replied in a gentle voice. Again he was looking for reassurance that she was going to respect his boundaries, and that she was not going to lead him someplace he did not wish to go. "I understand that you don't want to be in therapy more than a few months, and I'll do whatever I can to help you accomplish your goals in that time. But realistically you never know how long something's going to take until you start to work on it."

The patient nodded and probed her with his anxious eyes. "And I don't want to talk about my childhood. I know you're an analyst and analysts always want you to talk about your childhood, but I really don't believe in all that, if you want to know the truth. I hope I'm not offending you when I say that."

"No, you're not offending me. Actually, I want to encourage you to always say whatever you're thinking or feeling about me, or about the therapy." She took the opportunity to begin educating him, a process that would be ongoing. "It's okay if you don't want to talk about your childhood. We'll work on whatever you think is important." She knew it would be best not to press the issue of childhood reconstruction now.

"I mean, I know people who've been in analysis all their lives, and they're still as messed up as ever. I really don't believe in psychoanalysis. I think Freud is outdated. I mean, what do you think?"

She felt a twinge of resentment, analyzed it as countertransference, and then spoke undefensively: "Actually, I don't think about Freud when I'm doing therapy. I'm only thinking of how to help the person in the room. I hear that you have reservations about Freud and that you don't want to talk about your childhood. I understand. I assure you I won't pressure you in any way to do anything you don't want to do." She smiled in a calming, nurturing way.

"That sounds good." The patient seemed somewhat reassured. "May I ask you some questions about yourself?"

"Certainly. What would you like to know?"

The patient asked her about her background and training—information he was entitled to know and which she gave to him without hesitation. He asked her about her method of working, and she again used the opportunity to educate him about the process, explaining in broad terms about how it would be his job to say whatever thoughts came into his head and her job to assist him in understanding those thoughts. She did not wish to tell him too much for she knew that would only arouse his resistances, which were already considerable. She kept the explanation to a minimum.

The patient's arms dropped to his sides and his gaze grew less probing as the session wore down. He looked more comfortable than when he had entered the office. The therapist had succeeded in assuaging his fears and doubts, which was the first order of business, and in establishing an initial contract—agreeing to work on a particular problem, for a limited period of time, without going into the patient's history. Of course, she knew that once they began working on the patient's audition fright, it would lead to other aspects of his life; but she would let him discover that for himself. Through her empathic listening and answers to his questions, she had demonstrated that she could hear him without judging him, that she was sympathetic to his concerns, that she had no need to guide him where he did not wish to go, and that she was open to criticism and negative feelings about herself or the therapy.

"You know, I felt really scared of coming here today," the patient confessed at the end of the session. "I don't know why, but I did. Now I feel glad I came. And relieved. In fact, I'm looking forward to our next session."

Intervention 2

The Patient Who Defeated Many Great Therapists

A middle-aged woman came for a therapeutic consultation with an elderly male therapist who had become wise over the years. The woman, who was short and muscular, spoke articulately and somewhat bitterly of her previous disappointments with therapists. "I've been to some of the most famous therapists in New York. I went to see a well-known psychiatrist who had written several books. I'm not going to mention his name. I'm sure you'd know him. Anyway, after three sessions I realized he was too pompous, too egoistic to really care about or help me. I told him so, and left." She related her encounters with other therapists, including a group therapy experience in which she had challenged the leader's handling of a termination by another member. "I thought she was being really critical of that young girl and was in fact causing harm to her, and I said so. Then I said if she was going to treat people in the group that way just because they wanted to leave that I would leave myself. And I did. She wrote me several letters and kept calling me and telling me to come back and stop acting like a baby. I never went back."

When she had come to the end of her tale, she stopped and gazed at the present therapist. She had moved one of his chairs right up to the recliner he occupied, and now she sat facing him, a glare in her eyes. "What do you think? Can you help me?"

"I can help you if you'll let me help you," he gently replied. He observed her guardedly, one of his white brows arched.

"I mean, can you *really* be there for me?" There was a tone of intimacy in her voice that was inappropriate to the situation, and a probing, challenging, pleading look in her eyes. "I just don't want you to turn out like my other therapists. They all started to dislike me after a while, and then they didn't care about me. I want to know that you'll really care about me and like me, no matter what."

The therapist felt a pulsation of fear and anger inside him, a response to the patient's unrealistic demands. He had an impulse to say, "What do you want from me?" but held the impulse in check, noting that it was a countertransference reaction. He waited a moment, then asked, "Suppose I said to you that I promise to always like you and care about you, no matter what. Would you believe me?"

"No."

"Then what could I do to convince you I won't turn out like your other therapists?"

"I don't know." She looked down and was silent.

The therapist studied her. He understood that she had already tried to defeat him by making a demand of him that he could not possibly meet. In effect, she had put him into a double-bind situation. If he had said he could not meet her demands, he would have proved his inadequacy; and if he had said he could meet them, he would have been lying and would also have proved his inadequacy. By utilizing the intervention of turning the question back to her, he was able to make her see for herself that her demand was unrealistic. He had seen many patients like her during his career, patients whose narcissistic rage and paranoia impelled them to attempt to defeat all those around them who they perceived as a threat. He had diagnosed her as an oral-sadistic personality, whose excessive demands to be "fed" harkened back to her primary fixation in the oral-sadistic stage. He knew she was struggling against the depressive position by means of a paranoid defense, and that there was probably also a defense against penis envy toward a transferred father or brother. He knew all these things in a glance and then dismissed them, acting instead from a well-seasoned instinct. "What are you thinking?" he asked the patient.

She sat looking downward, a sad expression in her eyes. "I don't know. I'm . . . thinking."

"Thinking? Ah, that's good."

"Why is that good?" She shot an angry glance his way.

"Because that means you've learned something." He smiled at her with respect and sympathy. She looked down again, avoiding his gaze. He kept smiling, knowing from her downward gaze she had become his patient.

Intervention 3

The Threatening Patient
and the Threatening Therapist

Sometimes a therapist must meet force with counterforce. Such was the case when a borderline young woman, during the beginning phase, began acting out both in her group and individual therapy sessions with her female therapist. She became habitually late to the group and generally attempted to undermine the therapist by challenging her interpretations. She also came late to her weekly individual sessions and often spoke of not wanting to be there. One day, after missing a group session because somebody had given her tickets to a play, she began her individual session with, "I was thinking to myself as I came here today that I really didn't want to be here, and that if you got angry with me about missing the group last night, I'd quit."

"That's funny," the therapist replied. "I was just wondering whether, in view of your absence from the group last night, I ought to terminate you from therapy."

The patient was silent for a few minutes, then went on to talk about another subject.

What happened? The therapist had met force with force. The patient, maneuvering for control, had made a threat, and the therapist had countered with a threat. The therapist knew that in working with patients caught up in preoedipal resistance patterns, interpretations did little good. Such patients are not amenable to reasoning. The therapist therefore mirrored the patient's behavior and by doing so demonstrated to her what she was doing and nullified the maneuver with an opposing maneuver. If the therapist had responded to this threat with silence, as is often the case, the patient might have felt that she had "silenced" the therapist and secured control to some extent. This might then have encouraged more resistance.

Intervention 4

The Silent Patient
and the Silent Therapist

A young man told his older male therapist that his wife had suggested he go into therapy. The young man spoke in a halting manner, taking a long time to say even the most ordinary things. When the therapist asked why the man's wife had suggested he go into therapy, the man paused for a few minutes before answering.

"I guess . . . because she gets frustrated with me."

"Why does she get frustrated with you?"

Again, it was a minute or two before he answered. "I suppose . . . well . . . she complains that I don't talk to her."

"You don't talk to her? At all?"

There was another pause. "No, I talk to her . . . but . . . well . . . she says I don't tell her how I'm thinking or feeling about things. I guess that's it. . . . I don't know."

The office was filled with the man's silence. The therapist could feel it inside his own body. Already, in the space of a few minutes, the therapist was starting to feel frustrated with the young man. It was a struggle just to get him to provide the basic facts about why he had come to therapy. The therapist's impulse was to say to the young man, "Come on, spit it out!" This, of course, would have been exactly the wrong thing to say.

The young man had had a smothering and autocratic mother who had so overwhelmed him as a boy that he had developed the habit of stuttering, as well as lapsing into silences. His father, a passive-feminine type, had also been dominated by the mother, and he could not offer the boy the kind of masculine model he needed in order to separate from the mother. Now, as a young adult, the patient had married a domineering woman much like his mother, and had once again developed the habit of lapsing into silences.

The therapist understood this and adopted an accepting attitude toward the patient's silences. In the first few sessions, the patient lay on the couch and complained frequently that nothing was coming to his head. There were many silences.

The therapist remained silent as well, joining the patient's resistance, trying to convey to the patient that it was perfectly all right with the therapist if the patient did not wish to talk. The therapist sat very still in his chair and waited.

"I can't think of anything to say," the patient said after a while. "My mind's a blank."

"That's perfectly all right," the therapist replied. "Sometimes it takes a while before people get used to this process."

Another silence. "My mind's still a blank."

"That's fine. Just take all the time you want."

The therapist was careful not to pressure the patient in any way. Instead of trying to get him to tell what he was thinking, the therapist concentrated on trying to make him feel comfortable. Occasionally he would inquire how the patient was feeling:—Was the couch comfortable? Was it too hot in the office? Too cold? Was there anything the therapist could do or say to make it easier for the patient? The patient always replied that he was comfortable, that the room was fine, and that the therapist was fine. Also the therapist would occasionally ask if the patient was aware of feeling any pressure about talking. The patient replied that he did feel a bit of pressure, but not that much. However, the therapist was careful not to say anything to the patient unless the patient spoke first.

"I still can't think of anything," the patient would say after another silence.

"How are you feeling? Is it warm enough in here?"

"Yes, it's fine, thank you."

Gradually the patient got the message that the therapist was not going to force him to say anything he did not want to say, and that the therapist was truly concerned about the patient's comfort and well-being. By joining the patient's resistance and mirroring his silence, the therapist provided the kind of accepting environment that he had lacked as a child, and still lacked in his marriage. As the patient grew more confident in the therapist's benevolence, his silences grew shorter and less frequent. The therapist's questions, which were intended to convey the therapist's concern about the patient's comfort as well as to let him know that it was fine for him to express critical thoughts, had succeeded in building the first bridge of trust. The patient began to talk about superficial matters—a minor irritation at work, getting stuck on the subway, sending a present to a friend he had not seen for a year. But at least he was talking.

It would be another six months before he would begin to talk about his wife. However, the therapist's initial interventions had succeeded in advancing him to the next stage, dissolving his need to lapse into complete silences.

Intervention 5

The Critical Patient
and the Explanatory Therapist

"We're not getting anywhere," a male patient frequently complained. "I don't think you really understand me. The things you say to me just don't make sense. You're not helping me."

These complaints had started after about a year of therapy, and had continued for several months. The patient, a balding young man in his late twenties, was stuck in what Hyman Spotnitz calls the "negative judgment resistance." He had had a father who had always made him feel inadequate. If the patient, as a boy, tried to help his father build a fence, the father would grab the hammer out of his hands and say, "Let me do it. You're not holding it right." Never would the father attempt to explain how a hammer was held. Now the patient was unconsciously treating the therapist in a similar manner, disparaging all the therapist's efforts without providing any information as to how the therapist could improve.

The therapist gradually broke the impasse by calling attention to the fact that the patient was using a negative judgment resistance. "Your negative judgment resistance is interfering with the therapy process," he explained to the patient. "It might

15

be best for you to put the negative judgments aside for a while, and concentrate instead on remembering more about your childhood."

"I've already talked about my childhood."

"Yes, but there are still lots of things you can't remember, and by talking about them more, additional memories may emerge."

The patient was resistant to such explanations and requests, but he reluctantly followed the therapist's suggestion. He recalled more memories of his relationship with his father, and his critical attitude toward the therapist abated for a time. When the critical attitude returned again a few weeks later, the therapist again explained about the negative judgment resistance and asked the patient to put it aside for the good of the therapy.

"I need your cooperation," the therapist said. "I can't help you unless I have your cooperation."

"But it's not working," the patient angrily replied. "We're not getting anywhere."

"It takes time."

"I haven't got time. I'm in pain. I want to get better soon."

"Tell me more about your father."

"I've told you everything I can remember."

"Tell me again."

"Why?"

"Because it's important for your therapy."

The patient began to talk about his father again, then his mother, then his sisters. Without acknowledging it to the therapist, he began to recall new material.

This cycle continued for several years, until such time as the patient was able to verbalize more and more of his aggressive feelings to the therapist. By not responding with anger to the patient's critical attitude, nor trying to interpret it, the therapist frustrated the patient's attempt to draw the therapist into a power struggle with him, while guiding him deeper into analysis. Eventually the fights over giving up the negative judgment resistance grew more heated, and the patient's transference came more to the surface, where it could slowly be analyzed.

Intervention 6

The Play Therapist
and the Child Who Screamed

The therapist, a sweet-faced older woman, had first seen the patient when she was 2 years old. At that point the patient had become disturbed by the fact that her mother was pregnant and she had taken to running about the house screaming screams that no mortal had ever dared to scream before—or so it seemed to her mother. The more her mother tried to stop her, the more she screamed. The therapist intervened by suggesting to the mother that she be more aware of how her pregnancy was affecting the child. After one visit, she sent them on their way. They did not return for fourteen years.

At the age of 16, the daughter was once again brought to see the therapist, and once again the visit was preceded by a screaming fit. She had screamed and carried on with the house-mother at school and had been sent home with the strong recommendation that she see a psychiatrist. So her parents had driven her to the therapist's office and the therapist had chatted with them briefly. The therapist then asked to interview their daughter in private.

"Do you mind if we play a little game while we talk?" the therapist asked the girl when they were alone.

"What kind of game?"

She told her about the game Doodles. She would make a doodle on a sheet of paper, and the girl would then finish the doodle. Then the girl would make a doodle and the therapist would finish it. The girl sat down at the table and seemed glad to start out with this game. She was an attractive young woman with straight brown hair down to her shoulders, a red plastic coat and a red belt tied around her black miniskirt. She looked and acted very much like an adolescent. They began playing the game. The therapist drew a circular doodle and the girl made it into a face with long hair, which she said was a boy's long hair, although the face could be of any sex. The therapist turned her doodle into a dancer, the girl turned the therapist's into a golf player; the therapist changed the girl's into a bird, and the girl changed the therapist's into a top hat. The game went on for a few minutes and the therapist studied the girl's doodles, interpreting to herself the elements of gender confusion in the doodles. Eventually the girl began to talk freely about what had brought her to the therapist.

"I've been having trouble at school for some time now. It's dumb. I'm always trying to make people like me, respect me, not make a fool of me. I mean, it's all right if I try to entertain people and they laugh. But I'm always sitting around wondering what people are thinking of me. Always trying to make a good impression." She spoke of her relationship with her mother. "I've never been able to talk with her. In fact, I'm always lying to her. That's another reason they sent me to you. They say I'm always lying. I suppose I am."

"How do you lie?" the therapist asked.

"Oh, if my mother asks if I cleaned my room, I'll say I did. And I lie at school, too, about work. I don't work hard. You see, last term I was happy, but this term I'm unhappy. Maybe I'm growing too quickly. I wish there were somebody I could talk to. But every time I trust somebody, they always betray me." She went on to describe an incident at school. The housemother had chastised her and her roommates for not keeping their sitting room straight. After the woman had walked out of the room, the patient had thrown a knife against the door. It made a loud noise, and the housemother returned. She asked if the patient had lost her senses. The patient lied and said she was trying to mend the door handle. The housemother told her to take off her ridiculous hat. The patient said, "No, why should I?" The housemother told her to take it off because she said so. At that point the patient began to yell, then to scream. The housemother told her to stop screaming and the patient screamed more loudly. She screamed and screamed and screamed.

The therapist remembered her first interview with this girl, 14 years earlier, and how she had been screaming at her mother. She noted that the girl had a great deal of ambivalence with respect to the regressive and progressive mechanisms that lead to independence, both then and now. She was stuck at the separation–individuation stage, having difficulty separating from her mother. Her mother had disillusioned her when she was 2, changing from a good mother to a bad mother. Now the patient was recreating that kind of relationship with others in her life—the friends in whom she had confided and who then had betrayed her, and of course the housemother.

"It must be a relief to you when you can express your anger that way," the therapist said, wanting to establish empathy before going on with her interpretation. "But actually it's not the mean housemother you hate. It's the good one who was understanding and dependable." The girl shook her head, perplexed. "Whenever somebody behaves in a good and understanding way toward you, you don't trust it. You test them, provoke them, to see if they'll really be true. When they react to your provocations by being nasty back to you, then you hate them. This is what happened in your relationship with your mother, after your baby brother was born."

At first the girl seemed not to understand. Then she showed that she did by remembering a boyfriend who had broken up with her. "This boy was so marvelous. I could depend on him with my life. He never let me down. He loved me so much. He still does. But my negative self tried to spoil the relationship. I tried not to like him, because I thought he'd just let me down sooner or later. And then one day he said to me, 'I've decided to stop seeing you for a while. It's too maddening.' I was shocked." She thought about it. "I suppose I do expect the worst of people, and then set it up that way."

"What about me?" the therapist asked. "You're confiding in me today. Do you think I'll also betray you?"

"I wouldn't think so. But maybe. I've enjoyed this, though, and I'd like to see you again."

"I'm sure it can be arranged."

"Marvelous."

The young woman went into psychoanalysis with the therapist, cooperating enthusiastically for the three years of the treatment. By the age of 21 she was doing well at a university and managing her life adequately in other respects. The therapist's initial intervention of playing a game with her had immediately established a rapport, allowing her to proceed with an interpretation that would usually have come much later. The play therapy had quickly sent the relationship into a deeper level of communication. That and the therapist's previous encounter with the patient at age 2 had served to bond them therapeutically and set the stage for a successful psychoanalysis.

Intervention 7

The Patient Who Demeaned Women

"I've lost count of the number of women who've rejected me," a 32-year-old man complained to his female therapist. "Women can be so cruel. Especially liberated women. Or, so-called liberated women. All of them seem to look down their noses at me. I'd like to form a meaningful relationship. I would. But . . . forget it. I mean, excuse me, but I really think a lot of liberated women are dirt-bags."

For the first several weeks of his therapy the patient rambled on in this manner. His therapist, who was a year or so older, found herself feeling more than a little annoyed at him. However, she understood that he was transferring his frustrating and rejecting images on her, and that because of this he distrusted her. The patient was actually expressing his fear of destroying her and of her retaliation. He needed reassurance from her that he could trust her and that she would not "look down her nose" at him and reject him.

His fear of her had been further exacerbated when, in his initial session, he had complimented her. "You're kind of good looking . . . for a therapist," he had said in a backhanded way. Extending this compliment had awakened his feelings and disrupted his armor, particularly since she had only responded with a smile. Since then he had spoken with increasing bitterness about women.

The therapist, taking note of this, decided to join his resistance. She waited for a pause in his ramblings, then said, "Yes, women can be awfully cruel at times."

"Do you really think so?"

"Yes, I do. It's not easy being a man."

The intervention had an immediate effect. He turned his head slightly away from her and fell silent. Sitting facing her, he gazed downward, averting his eyes for a while. When he looked up, his face had softened considerably.

"I always feel it's me," he confided. "It's my fault. That's the way my mother always made me feel. Like it was me. She was always saying that no woman would put up with me . . . ."

Intervention 8

The Tired Therapist
and the Tired Patient

A young woman had been in therapy for several months with an older woman therapist. She had developed an idealizing transference of the twinship variety (Kohut), which stemmed from a fixation in the oral stage, during which she had idealized and felt a twinship with her mother. At this stage, everything her mother had thought, said, or felt, the patient likewise thought, said, and felt. Now this process had come into play in her therapy relationship.

One day the patient entered the office looking fresh and animated as usual, and took her seat facing the therapist. She spoke for fifteen minutes, then seemed to run out of energy. "I feel tired," she said, sighing. "I don't know why."

The therapist, noting the sudden resistance, proceeded to investigate by questioning her. "What do you think happened to make you tired?"

"Well, I woke up a little early this morning."

"Earlier than you did last week, or the week before that?"

"No, not really. I don't know. Maybe it's the weather."

"What about the weather?"

"It's hot outside, don't you think?"

"Yes, but in here it's cool."

"I don't know what it is."

"Maybe it was something that happened since you entered the office. Something I did or said."

There was a pause. "No, it wasn't anything you did . . . or said . . . ." The patient looked at the therapist apologetically. "I mean, not exactly. Actually, I just thought of something, but I'm embarrassed to tell you."

"Then you absolutely must tell me."

"Well, it's just . . . I don't know if this is it or not . . . but when I walked into the office today I thought to myself that you looked tired. But I didn't want to tell you, because I didn't want to make you feel uncomfortable."

The questioning technique, used so well by Socrates, is quite often the best intervention in today's therapy offices.

Intervention 9

The Abandoning Therapist

"Oh, by the way," a handsome male therapist said to his slightly overweight and somewhat dowdy female patient. "I'm going to be away on Friday, two weeks from today, so I'll have to cancel our session."

"That's fine," the patient replied, nodding sweetly.

But it was not fine. When the patient came for her next session, she was silent and withdrawn.

"What's the matter?" the therapist asked.

The patient lay on the couch, her face turned away from the therapist. She cleared her throat but did not speak.

"Are you angry at me about something?"

Silence.

Then it occurred to the therapist that the patient might be angry about his announcement that he would have to cancel a session. In fact, he had noticed a change in her facial expression when she had left his office the preceding session, and he had felt a twinge of guilt. He had made a mental note to follow up on the exchange during the next session. Now that session had come and he was confused by her silence. In analyzing her resistance and the anger behind it, he speculated that it might be the transference revival of the archaic experience of the bad breast, or the loss of the mirroring self-object, or the frustrating or rejecting oedipal father. He also understood that she felt inferior to men, particularly attractive men in good physical shape (which he was), so that she would experience any "rejection" by him all the more keenly. However, he knew she was not ready to hear an interpretation.

"You know, I feel bad," he told her.

After a moment of silence she asked, "What about?"

"I was just remembering last week when I told you I was going to cancel an appointment. I feel bad about having told you that at the end of the session, when there was no time for us to discuss it."

"Yes," the patient spoke up. "I did feel a little annoyed about that. You seemed to spring it on me so suddenly."

"I'm sorry about that." He waited a bit to let the apology sink in. "What other thoughts have you had about the incident? Did it bring up other feelings about me? Any memories from the past?"

With that, the patient launched into a monologue about how her mother had "abandoned" her in a nursery school when she was 2½-years-old. By mirroring the patient and showing that he understood and cared about her, and by expressing a negative feeling himself (thereby giving her permission to do so as well), the therapist had drawn her out of her withholding pattern.

Intervention 10

A Delayed Success

Sometimes a therapist will not know whether an intervention has been successful until a later date. Interventions do not always elicit an immediate response from the patient or bring about an immediate improvement. Occasionally an intervention may even seem to fail, and then at some future point there is response or improvement.

A young man of a borderline character constellation with features of paranoia, hypochondria, anxiety, and various phobias was advised by his therapist to go into group therapy after several years of individual therapy. The young man reluctantly did so. For the first two years in the group he complained nearly every week that he felt like quitting because the group was too threatening for him. His family had been a highly psychogenic environment in which nobody had modeled a healthy way of interacting or expressing feelings. Whenever the therapist attempted to get the patient to express his honest thoughts and feelings about a group member, or have them do so to him, he was highly resistant.

"I know what you're trying to do," he would tell the therapist, "but I'm sorry, I just can't do it."

Eventually he insisted on dropping out of the group, and the therapist went along with it. The therapist, a self psychologist, felt he needed to be understanding of the patient's fears. It appeared that the group therapy experience had been a failure, but the therapist knew in the back of his mind that it had been helpful, even if the patient did not realize it. The therapist was not surprised when the patient came to a session six months later and asked to join the group again.

"You know, I realized this weekend how much the group helped me. I was having a discussion with my girlfriend this weekend—or trying to have a discussion—about our relationship. And it dawned on me how much she acts out her feelings, and I found myself trying to teach her to verbalize her feelings like we did in the group."

Intervention 11

The Physician Who Spoke
with Medical Tongue

A physician was prone to using medical jargon as a defense against deeper thoughts and feelings. His therapist, an older man who used classical analytic technique, let him go on for several months without interpreting. The therapist did not wish to antagonize the patient by attacking a way of speaking with which the patient identified, and which constituted a narcissistic extension of his ego-ideal.

One day the physician began complaining in stilted tones that his wife had developed a problem. "She has developed this painful protruding tumor in her ovarian ligament," he said with calm resignation. "Naturally this had to happen prior to our mountain trip, and I must say it has caused me unmixed displeasure. I'm wondering now whether the tumor can be surgically excised, or whether we will in fact have to postpone our holiday."

The therapist, sensing the latent anger the patient was withholding, suddenly spoke out in a deliberately angry way himself: "I think you really mean your wife's tumor is a pain in the ass."

The patient replied without hesitation, as though waiting for just such a prompting: "That's right, you son of a bitch, I wish they would just cut out both her ovaries and get it over with. I can't stand these women and their constant female problems that interfere with my sex life." With that he launched into a diatribe about his mother's hysterectomy when he was 6-years-old, which precipitated an infantile neurosis.

It is not just the content of an interpretation that is important, but also the timing and the tone of voice with which it is delivered. In this instance all three—the content, the timing, and the tone of voice—were instrumental in the interpretation's success.

Intervention 12

The Seductive Patient
and the Novice Therapist

From the first time she walked into his office, the therapist could feel a powerful current of sexual feelings inside him. Indeed, the feelings seemed to permeate the entire office while she was present. She was a classical hysteric, a beautiful woman from Hungary, whose expressions and posture and tone of voice oozed sexuality. There was always on her face the trace of a smirk, as though she were thinking, "Yes, I know I'm quite attractive and I know you want my body, but you won't have it." Her every gesture was a provocation, every flicker of her eyes—which were blue and gazed knowingly downward—was a challenge.

"I don't know why it always has to be that way," she said to the therapist in her sensual Hungarian accent. She was referring to her relations with men. "I don't know why there always has to be that sexual thing, right from the beginning. Why can't we just be friends? It's always the same thing. As soon as they meet me they want to go to bed with me."

"Why do you think they want to go to bed with you right away?" her novice therapist asked.

"Because that's the way men are. That's the way my father

was. He was always womanizing. And my older brother, too. That's all they think about."

"And you think all men are this way? Without exception?"

"I don't know. I suppose there are exceptions, but I've never met any."

"And what about me? I'm a man."

"So?"

"I haven't asked you to go to bed with me."

"Of course not. You're a therapist."

"And if I weren't a therapist?"

"Then you would have asked me to go to bed with you by now."

The theme of her sessions always centered on men's demands for sex, and the therapist, attempting to analyze both the patient's seductivity—of which she was primarily unaware—and his own substantial erotic countertransference—of which he was painfully aware—could not find a way to break the impasse. The patient had both an obsession with, and an aversion toward, sex. The obsession was with something forbidden, harkening back to archaic events in her childhood that pertained to her first discoveries of her genitalia, which were met with disapproval by her mother. The aversion stemmed from penis envy, which she had felt most strongly toward her older brother, who was favored by her mother. To have sex with a man meant to her not only having sex with her brother (having his despised penis inside her), but also stirring the jealousy and wrath of her mother for doing something sexual and forbidden. Transferentially, the therapist was now this admired and envied brother.

Knowing all this did not help him find the right intervention, as he was both a novice and smitten by countertransference feelings and therefore unable to think clearly. The patient continued to resist analysis. She refused to lie on the couch, claiming it was a way for the therapist, a man, to get her into a horizontal position. She avoided talking about her childhood for the most part, and scarcely spoke of anything except her relationships with men currently in her life. And she continued to behave seductively toward the therapist. She would sit facing him, the ever-present smirk at the corners of her mouth, head slightly bent, glancing up at him every now and then to check out his state of sexual excitement. Whenever the therapist attempted to analyze her relationships with men, or with him, she would brush his attempts aside. She spoke quickly at these times, reacting out of her fear of hearing the truth.

The therapist spoke about the case with his supervisor, a modern psychoanalyst. The supervisor pointed out that the patient had, in a sense, sexually conquered the therapist. He alluded to her remark that if the therapist were not a professional he "would have asked me to go to bed with you by now." "You see," the supervisor said, "she thinks she already has you, and because of that she has contempt for you. And as long as she has contempt for you, she won't take you seriously as a therapist. You could have used that statement as an opportunity to set her straight, or to at least give her some doubts. You might have asked her, 'Are you sure?' Or you could have explained to her that even though you might be sexually attracted to her, you wouldn't act on that feeling because you knew it wouldn't work out. She'd then ask why it wouldn't work out, and you'd tell her you experience her as being out of touch with her feelings, particularly her sexual and aggressive feelings, and therefore she wouldn't be capable of relating to you the way you'd want a woman to relate. By telling her these things you'd be giving her a motive to want to work out her problems, and you'd be modeling a mature way of being. She'd get angry at you and want to seduce you even more, but she'd also start to understand her transference and to separate you from her brother and from other men."

"The problem is," the therapist replied, "I'm not sure I could really say to her that I wouldn't act out my sexual feelings if I weren't her therapist."

"Then lie," the supervisor said.

The therapist waited for another opportunity to arise. He did not have to wait long. During her next session, the young woman again brought up her difficulties with men, and the therapist asked her if she experienced the same difficulty with respect to him.

"You're different," she replied. She smirked and looked down. "You're a therapist."

"I'm also a man."

"Yes, I know." She smiled knowingly.

"And yet I haven't made a pass at you."

"Because you're a therapist."

"And if I weren't a therapist?"

"Then I'm sure you would."

"Why are you sure?"

"Well, maybe I shouldn't assume things."

"Maybe you shouldn't."

The smirk left her mouth. "I don't know what you're driving at. What's this got to do with my problem? Why are you always bringing yourself into this?"

"Because I'm trying to show you something. You assume that all men are the same, they all want to make love to you. But that's not true in my case. I'm sexually attracted to you, but I don't want to make love to you."

"Oh?" She looked up. The smirk had changed to a puzzled smile. "All right. I'll bite. Why not?"

"Because I don't think it would work out. I don't think you're in touch with your sexual or aggressive feelings, and I wouldn't feel safe with you."

"Oh, I see." The puzzled smile froze for an instant. Then she cocked her head and put her hands on her hips. "What do you mean, I'm not in touch with my sexual and aggressive feelings? That sounds like a bunch of psychoanalytic gobbledegook to me!"

"Does it?"

"Yes, it certainly does."

The analytic dialogue had begun. The therapist had gotten her to begin to look at her interaction with the therapist by challenging and confronting her. This would lead to discussions and insights about her relationships in general, including her past relationships with primary figures.

Intervention 13

The Self-Sacrificing Patient

A young woman had developed a certain kind of resistance to therapy after a few months. She would lapse into long silences, then begin asking her therapist, a man of about her own age, questions about his personal life. "How is your wife? How are your children? Do you go out much? What was your childhood like? Was it happy or sad?"

The therapist knew there was avoidance of some kind going on, and that he had to get to it in a delicate way, without unduly frustrating the patient. "I appreciate your concerns about me," he told her one day, "and at some point I'll be glad to answer these questions. However, at the present time I'm more interested in finding out why you would want to replace therapeutic curiosity about yourself with concern about my personal affairs and welfare."

"That's an interesting point," the patient replied. "I never thought of that."

Through his caring observation, which constituted a mirroring of her own concern for him, he was able to arouse her curiosity about her own process and eventually demonstrate to her that the anxiety she felt in her dealings with him was behind her silence and her questions about his personal life.

The patient had been brought up to live the life of a self-sacrificing person. As a result, she had developed intense feelings of resentment against those who had forced this self-sacrificing role upon her—parents, siblings, and friends. Her kindness became a reaction formation to the resentment and the destructive fantasies associated with it. Eventually she had become stuck in the obsessional pattern of evading any personal questions she was asked—whether by relatives, friends, or strangers—by asking a personal question that expressed concern about the questioner. In succeeding sessions, this pattern and the childhood events that had led to it was finally explored.

Intervention 14

The Overzealous New Patient

Impulsive personality types will often enter therapy on the heels of a crisis and will seem ready to dedicate their lives to therapy. One such patient, who came to therapy after his girlfriend left him because of his alcoholism and abusive behavior, was the prototype of this variety of humanity. "I can't go on like this," he said to his female therapist, shaking his head, eyeing her with the utmost earnestness and remorse. "I've got to do something and I know it. I need to get in touch with my feelings. There's a lot of anger inside me, and I keep taking it out on my girlfriend, and it makes me drink and it's destroying my life. Do you do primal therapy? I think I need to really get into my feelings. And I also think I need to come more than twice a week. Maybe three times a week. I really want to lick this problem. I really do. What do you think?" He looked at her with the meek, pitiful eyes of a child.

"What do I think about what?" she asked in a voice and manner of calmness that was a counterpoint to the young man's desperation.

"Do you do primal therapy? I'd like to get right in touch with my feelings."

The therapist did not answer right away. Her temptation

was to pull out a mat and let him go to it, so strong was the energy she felt coming from him. Yet she held back, knowing from experience that he was not really committed to getting in touch with and working through his feelings. Unconsciously, he wanted to draw the therapist into a power struggle; he would make her into his surrogate mother (a role his girlfriend had now relinquished), pretending he was ready to be the perfect patient, thereby gratifying his mother's desire for him to be an obedient son. Were the therapist to go along with this charade and allow him to do primal therapy and come three times a week, she would find him suddenly change direction. As abruptly as he had thrown himself into therapy he would want to leave it. Underlying this impulsiveness was his resentment toward his parents and toward all parental surrogates.

"No," she finally answered. "I don't do primal therapy, and anyway I don't think it would be right for you." She spoke in a gentle, firm way.

"Oh?" He was taken aback, expecting that she, like other women, would fall for his boyish appeal for help. "Why not?"

"Because I think what you need right now is to get some control over yourself. You're out of control. As you said, you keep doing things to destroy your life. The first thing we need to do is to help you get control over your drinking and over your behavior toward your girlfriend."

The young man looked at her angrily. "I see. And how do I do that?" There was noticeable resentment in his voice.

"First of all, before we even start therapy I'd require you to enroll in a self-help program such as Alcoholics Anonymous. It's been my experience that unless somebody with a drinking problem has stopped drinking, therapy is of little use."

"I can stop drinking without AA."

"I don't doubt your sincerity, but my experience has proved otherwise."

The young man proceeded to argue with the therapist about

it. She listened silently to his arguments. At the end he said, "I'll have to think about this!"

"All right. Take your time." She smiled in a caring way. "I'll give you my card, and if you wish to take me up on my offer, just give me a call."

"I'll do that!"

The young man left the office in a huff. Whether he would return or not was unimportant. The therapist's intervention—frustrating his impulsivity and explaining the realities of the situation—would be invaluable to him in any case. He had met an authority figure who had responded in a healthy way and shown him the path required of him. Whether he took that path with her or—after another crisis—with another therapist, at least the path had been laid down for him.

Intervention 15

The Patient Who Wanted Advice

A young man kept asking his older male therapist for advice. "I'm not sure what to do about my career," he would say. "Some friends of mine suggested I go into computer graphics, but I don't know. Then I'd feel I wasted my time getting a teaching degree. But the thought of being a teacher makes me sick. My mother wants me to go to medical school. Forget that. I don't know. What do you think I should do?"

For a time, the therapist kept answering all such requests for advice with the explanation, "I don't give advice. I don't think it would be helpful to you if I advised you, for I feel it's important that you come to your own decisions."

Each time he was given this explanation, the young man nodded and seemed to understand. However, a session or two later he would once again solicit advice. He had been brought up in a family in which he had never been allowed to make decisions for himself. Both his parents as well as his older sister criticized and sometimes ridiculed his choices in clothing, friends, hobbies, and the like. The only way he could get any approval in this environment was to solicit advice from them, which they were only too happy to give him but which he never followed. When he did take their advice and try something they recommended, he would inevitably sabotage it. When he made a choice that he knew they would disapprove of, he would also sabotage it. Hence he was always in a state of indecision.

"What should I do? What should I do?" the young man kept asking.

The therapist, in order to break the stalemate, decided to change his tactic. "Well, you could try being a teacher and see how it goes."

"That's true," the patient answered, delighted to get this advice.

"Or you could try the computer graphics."

"That's a good idea."

"Or you could try applying to some medical schools."

"I could."

"Or you could go into advertising. You've talked about that at times."

"Yes . . . I've talked about that." His delight was fading.

"Or you could try all four in succession. And then choose."

"I never thought about that."

"Or you could train to be an airline pilot. You like traveling."

"An airline pilot? That takes a long time." He had started wondering what was up.

"Then again, I heard the fingernail clipper factory in Brooklyn is hiring."

"I don't get it."

"I'm giving you advice."

"I know, but it's too much advice. And it's . . . weird."

There was a long silence.

"What are you thinking?" the therapist asked.

The patient lay on the couch, gazing toward the wall. "I'm thinking that your advice isn't helpful. In fact, *advice* isn't helpful. I have to decide for myself. I have to make up my own mind. But I can't." He tossed around, crossing and uncrossing his legs, cracking his neck, stretching his arms. The therapist had saturated him with advice and had thereby demonstrated to him the inanity of the situation, forcing him to a deeply felt conclusion. "Why can't I make up my mind?" he asked plaintively.

"That's what we have to analyze. Why you can't make up your mind."

The patient signed and nodded.

Intervention 16

The Narcissistic Transference

In the beginning phase of therapy, narcissistic patients are not yet capable of establishing an object transference with the therapist—that is, they do not see the therapist as a person separate from themselves. Fixated in the first two years of life, they tend to focus on themselves and they develop a narcissistic transference toward the therapist, making him or her an extension of themselves. The task of the therapist in such cases is to get the patient to establish an object transference; one way of doing this is to continually direct the patient's attention away from himself or herself and toward the therapist.

A depressed 30-year-old man used to spend nearly every session complaining about the various things that were wrong with him. "I feel so angry all the time. I don't know why. And I'm always so self-conscious. I think people are always thinking what a fat slob I am. I hate my body. I hate the fact that I'm always having trouble with my, you know, sexual organs. I never feel comfortable anywhere. And nothing seems to help. Nothing."

The therapist began asking the patient object-oriented questions (that is, questions that directed the patient's attention to the therapist as a separate object).

"Have I been making you angry?"

"No."

"Do I make you feel self-conscious?"

"No . . . well, a little."

"Do you think *I* think you're a fat slob?"

"I don't know. Maybe, sometimes."

"When do you think I'm thinking that?"

"When I walk into the office."

"And when you leave?"

"Yes, when I leave, too."

"Am I helping you?"

"Helping me what?"

"Feel more comfortable?"

"I don't know. I don't know. I don't know."

The object-oriented questions were irritating to the patient, for he had long defended against establishing real contact with another human. However, such questions would eventually turn his attention outward, and his aggression could then be analyzed.

Intervention 17

The Crazy Patient
and the Crazy Therapist

"I've got a new idea," the patient said. He was a schizophrenic who liked to develop new ideas for getting rich every other week. "Listen to this," he told his therapist, a young woman who had grown skeptical. "This idea is going to make me rich, for sure. You know how women are always saying they wish they could pee standing up, like men? I got to thinking about that, and I started drawing some designs. Take a look at these." He handed her some poorly drawn designs of objects that resembled funnels, with suction cups at the large end. "You see, with this artificial penis, women can pee standing up. All they have to do is press the suction cup around their vagina and they've got a penis." He conveyed this idea to her, as usual, in a monotone. "Women all over the world will be buying them. It'll be bigger than the Hoola-hoop."

"I've got an even better idea," the therapist said. "How about designing it so that the penis actually gets erect and ejaculates real sperm? This would enable women to impregnate each other, so they wouldn't have to depend on men. Think of the lesbians all over the world who'd buy it."

"You know, Doctor," the patient replied, "sometimes I think you're a real crackpot."

By "outcrazying" the patient—using exaggerated mirroring—the therapist had accomplished four aims. She had gotten the patient to notice her as a separate object; she had provoked his anger and shown him that it was all right for him to express it to her; she had conveyed the notion that not only her own, but the patient's idea was absurd; and she had demonstrated that if she, with her crazy ideas, could function successfully in the world, then so might he.

Intervention 18

The Patient Who Brought a Gift

A young man brought his male therapist a gift – a mask that he had purchased during a trip abroad. "I thought you might like this," he said, handing it to the therapist, "being that you collect them."

The therapist took it into his hands and looked it over. It was of carved wood, with delicate brushwork across the face in primary colors. The therapist would have liked very much to add this mask to his collection, but the feelings that came up inside him made him pause. He did not have a rule about not accepting gifts from patients, but in this case it did not feel right. "I appreciate the thought very much," he said, "but I'm afraid I can't accept it."

"Oh? Why?" The patient, who sat facing the therapist, was clearly upset. His brows turned down between his dark eyes and he looked at the therapist demandingly.

"I can't accept it because it would be bad for your therapy," the therapist said. "Believe me, I'd like to take it. It's a fine mask, and I don't wish to hurt your feelings. But I'm convinced it would be the wrong thing to do – it would contaminate our relationship. I especially think it might be destructive because of where you are right now in your therapy, and I think it's important that we analyze why you want to give it to me."

The patient, who had been in therapy only a few months, was too disappointed to do much analyzing that session, but during the following session he began to talk of his homosexual fears and fantasies.

"Actually," he confessed, "I didn't really want you to accept the gift. It was a test to see whether you could be seduced—I realized it as soon as I left your office." He added that the therapist's refusal of the gift had communicated the message that the therapist could not be seduced and that it was therefore safe for the patient to talk about his homosexual feelings, which he had been warding off until then. "I used to try to win my father's approval all the time, sometimes by buying him gifts. I always felt he was angry at me, I guess because of the way Mom was always fawning over me. But the thing is, I think I had contempt for him whenever he took one of my gifts. Yeah, I know I had contempt for him. I know I did. . . ." He looked up at the therapist. "It's amazing how afraid I was to talk about all this."

Intervention 19

The Gestalt Therapist
and the Multiple Personality

Sometimes an intervention will achieve unexpected results. Such was the case when a therapist, utilizing a Gestalt therapy orientation, asked his depressed young female patient to role-play. She had been in treatment for several months, was suicidal, and complained of the futility of life.

"You sound very pessimistic," he told her.

"I am."

"Do you have an optimistic part of you?" He looked at her for a moment. She sat wanly in the chair facing him, rocking slightly to and fro, hugging herself. "Do me a favor. Sit in that chair over there." He pointed to an empty chair next to her. "Sit in that chair and be your optimistic self."

"My optimistic self?"

"That's right."

She gazed at the chair, puzzled and sad, then arose and sat in it. She sat stiffly at first, looking down at her lap, sighing. Her hands came up over her face as though she were about to cry. When her hands fell away, she sat back and there was a completely different expression on her face. Even the shape of her face was different. "Hello," she said, smiling confidently.

"Are you your optimistic self?" the therapist asked.

"That's me." She gazed at him with a striking boldness. "My name's Janet. Nice to meet you."

The therapist had accidently stumbled upon one of the patient's six alter-personalities.

Intervention 20

Telephone Call
from a Prospective Patient

"Hello. I was referred to you by a friend of mine, Cynthia Green."
It was a young woman's voice with a nervous, submissive quality.

"Yes," the therapist answered in a calm, friendly tone.
"What can I do for you?" She was a female therapist in her fifties.

"I think I'm interested in therapy."

"All right."

"With a woman therapist."

"Last time I checked I was a woman."

A nervous giggle. "Cynthia said you were very good. But
she didn't say what kind of therapy you did or what your,
you know, philosophy was. Could you tell me something about
yourself?"

"What would you like to know?" The therapist had begun to
feel wary of the young woman; her submissiveness did not seem
real, and her line of questioning was too broad. "It would be best
if you asked a specific question."

"Well, I don't know. I have trouble articulating things . . . I
guess that's one reason I need a therapist. I mean, the reason I
wanted to see a woman therapist is because I'm really angry at

men right now. Actually, I was wondering if you're a feminist. Would you describe yourself as a feminist therapist?"

"What would it mean to you if I said I was?"

"I don't know. I guess it would mean we're on the same wavelength."

"Is it important for us to be on the same wavelength?"

"You're not going to answer my question, is that it?"

"My policy is not to answer personal questions," the therapist replied firmly but in a friendly way. The woman's tone of voice had begun to irritate the therapist. In analyzing her own feelings, she realized the woman was putting her in a double-bind situation with her line of questions. If she said she was not a feminist, the patient would reject her; if she said she was, the patient might distrust the therapist's sincerity, assuming she had manipulated her into saying so. "I only answer questions about my educational background and training," the therapist added.

"Oh. I see." The woman on the phone seemed momentarily derailed. "All right. Yes, what is your background?"

"Can you ask a specific question?"

"Yes, yes. Are you a psychologist?"

"No. I'm a Certified Social Worker."

"I see. I was kind of interested in seeing, you know, somebody with a Ph.D. I hope I'm not offending you."

"No, you're not. If you want somebody with a Ph.D. I can refer you to my partner."

"She has a Ph.D.?"

"Yes, she does."

"That's an idea. . . ." The woman's voice trailed off, and there was another pause. "Well, may I ask you one other question? It's about your method of working. You *do* answer questions about that, don't you?" An edge of sarcasm had crept into her voice.

"Go ahead."

"Well, I'd kind of like to work with somebody who, you know, believes in past-life therapy. Somebody who does hypnosis."

The therapist studied this last question for a moment. It was apparent that this young woman, through her inordinate demandingness, was out to either control or reject her. It also seemed apparent that the woman was prone to splitting, and the sarcasm in her voice indicated that she now saw the therapist as a "bad mother" because she had failed to supply the narcissistic necessities (agreement/milk/approval). If the therapist/mother would not give her what she wanted, immediately, she would destroy her—causing her to feel inadequate by making demands she could not meet. The therapist decided it was not possible to get this patient into therapy with her, but she chose an intervention—joining the resistance and countering her questions with her own—which might nevertheless push her into therapy with somebody else. "Let me see," she said, calmly and seriously. "You're looking for a woman therapist who's a feminist, who has a Ph.D., and who does past-life therapy and hypnosis. Is that correct?"

"Yes."

"All right. Are there any other requirements?"

"Actually, I was also kind of hoping to find somebody who was, you know, Jewish."

"Orthodox or Reformed?" the therapist quickly shot back.

"I hadn't thought about that . . . . Are you making fun of me?"

"Why would I make fun of you?"

"I don't know. Maybe, maybe you think I'm being a little too demanding."

"Why would I think that?"

"People are always telling me I'm demanding, but I'm *not.*" Her tone had suddenly become strident. "I'm really not. I just know what I want and I assert myself. That's not being demanding. That's self-assertion." There was another pause. "I think maybe I'd better call another therapist."

"All right."

Intervention 21

The Patient Who Wanted Sole Possession of Her Therapist

"Usually, I don't want to come to therapy," the young woman told her female therapist. "And when I do come, I don't want to know that you have other patients. Maybe that's why I often come late. I don't want to see another patient leave your office. I'd like to think that you belong to me." The patient stopped and lay thoughtfully on the couch for a few minutes. Then she asked, "What do you make of that?"

The therapist did not answer right away. Even though the patient was asking for an interpretation, she had to decide whether the patient was ready for an interpretation and, if so, how it should be worded. She had been in therapy for only about six months; however, she seemed to have a fairly strong ego. And the fact that she was asking for an interpretation seemed to signal, at the very least, the start of an object transference. In reviewing the patient's background, the therapist recalled that she had been displaced in her mother's and father's attention by the birth of her younger sister. The only adult who had been available to her was a governess, and the patient had developed a possessive, clinging relationship to this woman. Obviously the patient was transferring the governess onto the therapist.

"Does this situation feel familiar?" the therapist asked. "The situation of wanting sole possession of somebody?"

"Not really," the woman answered at first. "Oh, I see. You want me to say that it reminds me of how I felt about Ellen," she added, referring to the governess by name. "But that's ridiculous. That was completely different . . . ." She quieted down and stretched out. "Then again, maybe you're right. There is a similarity in the way I feel about you and the way I felt about her. Of course, I know very well that my seeing this does not mean it's gone, but at least I understand it, and that's the first step."

Intervention 22

The Therapist Who Had
a Resistant Group

The group had been acting out resistance from the very beginning of its formation a few months earlier. The members of the
group, primarily high-powered business people, did not make the
group a priority in their lives. There was a high degree of
absenteeism, so that although there were six members, on occasion only two or three would show up. Those who did not show up
always had excellent excuses, related to their businesses.

The therapist brought the matter to his supervisor. "I feel
like I just want to throw in the sponge," he exclaimed. "Either
that or strangle a few of them." Upon analyzing the situation, it
turned out that the therapist was charging a very high fee for the
group, higher than he had ever charged before. This had made
him, unconsciously, more than usually concerned that the group
be a success, for it meant a considerable rise of his income. He
also felt some guilt about charging so much, and this caused him
to be oversolicitous. As the therapist discussed these factors, he
realized that the group members had most likely picked up on his
guilt feelings and his need for group success. Hence, the group
had become "his" group, rather than theirs, and they had begun
acting out their resentment toward the leader who was getting

rich at their expense. "Now that I understand it, how do I set things right?" the therapist asked.

It was July—nearly time for the August break. "I'd suggest you say the following to your group when they meet again," the supervisor said. "Tell them there seems to be a problem with respect to members attending the group—but don't go into any analysis because I don't think they're ready for that. Just say there seems to be a problem, and since it's nearly time for the summer break, perhaps they should break early and give people time to straighten out their business affairs and decide if they really want the group. Tell them you'll make an appointment in the fall, and when they meet again they can discuss whether they want to continue or discontinue the group."

The therapist followed the supervisor's suggestion. When the group returned in the fall, group members were unanimous in wanting to continue the group, and absenteeism virtually ceased. By joining their resistance, the therapist conveyed that he did not need the money and that it really was their group, to build or to destroy.

Intervention 23

The Art Therapist

She had been seeing her therapist twice a week for nearly a year when the therapy hit an impasse. Each session would start in the same way.

"What should we do today?" she would ask, yawning.

"What would you like to do?"

"I'd like not to be here."

She was an attractive woman of about thirty, quite intelligent and witty in a somewhat caustic way, who had been struggling for many months with unresolved anger toward her mother. She was a writer who could not write, and although she knew her writer's block was somehow connected with her mother's ridicule of not only her writing but also any other intellectual pursuit, the anger remained unresolved because it had become transferred onto the therapist, a man who was about her same age. Not only had her mother ridiculed her achievements, she also made her feel guilty if she had any negative feelings about her. As a result, the brunt of her rage was directed at her father, a passive man, and to men in general. On an archaic level, she longed for a father figure who would rescue her from her prohibitive oedipal mother and who would allow her to separate from her. In her mind, the therapist had become another passive, depriving father figure who had failed her. However, she was as yet unable to acknowledge any of this to herself.

In the months preceding the impasse, as more and more of her transference anger surfaced, her life outside the therapy office had become increasingly problematic. She had been having serious fights with her husband, and she had a series of "accidents," the most recent of which involved a bicycle crash leaving her sprained and bruised and hospitalized. The day after she got out of the hospital she had called the therapist and wanted to know if he would make a house call.

"It's my policy not to make house calls," he explained. She had been seductive toward him and he felt a house call, under the circumstances, would be tantamount to giving in to her seduction, as well as to an ongoing narcissistic demandingness. "I'll do a telephone session with you, though," he added.

"No, that's all right," she snapped. "I'll just have to wait until I'm able to come to the office. I don't know when that will be."

It was the therapist's refusal to do the house call that brought on the impasse. After that she was aloof, moody, and more caustic than usual. The message was that if he would not give her what she wanted, she would not give him what he wanted—that is, she would not be a cooperative patient. She was not amenable to interpretations, questions, or other interventions. Her sessions were full of silences and yawns and complaints about boredom. Several weeks passed in this vein.

The therapist decided to use art therapy techniques as a way to break the impasse. In addition to being a writer, she also painted as a hobby and had shown an interest in art from an early age. He reasoned that having her draw might be the vehicle that would open her up to his interpretations. Since she complained of being bored by the usual routine of therapy, this joining of her resistance might help her break out of that routine.

When he broached the subject of the drawings, she was flippant. "You want me to draw pictures? Why not? Do you think it will cure me?" She shot him a crooked grin.

"I think it might provide us with some insights."

"Oh, good. I love insights."

She did some pencil drawings in an offhanded manner, smiling all the while as though it were a joke. One drawing was of a house, a tree, and a woman standing under the tree. When she had finished, the therapist picked up this drawing and studied it. Her penciling was quite light, and there was a considerable amount of white space. He thought, without telling the patient, that the smallness of the drawing and the abundance of white space were indicative of regression in a hostile environment. The hostile environment not only pertained to her childhood, but also, through transference, to the therapy office, onto which she had projected her aggression. In the drawing and in life she had regressed to a preoedipal defensive posture.

"Well," she said. "What do you think, Doctor? How sick am I?"

"Do you really want to hear my interpretations, or is that a rhetorical question?"

"Sure. Let's hear it. Do I have a choice?"

"Of course you have a choice. You always have a choice."

"All right. I'm game." She smiled suspiciously.

"Are you sure?"

"I'm sure."

He spoke slowly and deliberately. "You see all this white space? You see how small you made your drawings, and how lightly you penciled them? That usually indicates withdrawal, lack of commitment, and repressed anger."

"I know all that. It's true. I'm not committed. I don't have any friends. I've withdrawn from everybody, including my husband. So? What else is new?"

"We don't have to do this if you don't want to."

"No, no. Go on. Tell me more about the drawings, so I can be enlightened and mature."

The therapist pointed to the clouds hovering over the roof, the blackness of the roof, and the smoke coming out of the chimney. "These are all signs of depression and anger." He pointed out that the house had not been drawn in proportion: one side was done from one perspective, whereas the back was done from another. "This is also an indication of repressed anger." Her tree had no roots. "You're not rooted." The branches of the tree were represented only by light lines, and there were but a few of them. "You haven't branched out very much; you haven't reached out. And the leaves are very gloomy and gray." The woman had a flat head. "That flat head says to me that you feel intellectually oppressed." The woman's eyes were looking fearfully to the left. "You seem afraid of the future." Her hands were hidden behind her back. "And you seem to be hiding something."

The therapist put the drawing down and studied her. She immediately sat up and smiled matter-of-factly.

"Very interesting. But what does it prove? I know all that already."

He sensed she was angry about the interpretations but, as usual, was not expressing it directly. "How do you feel about what I've said?"

"It gives me something to think about. Yes, I'll think about it. Is that what I'm supposed to do?"

She was always asking him what she was supposed to do. "No," he answered, "it's not what you're supposed to do. But if you want to think about it, you may."

"Thank you, Doctor. I'll think about it, then."

She did not mention the drawings during the next session, or the one after that, or the one after that. Once again the impasse had seemingly settled in, and now the silence with regard to her response to the drawings became a part of the impasse. He did not wish to bring up the subject first, as she had

a tendency to feel coerced by him whenever he initiated anything. Finally, after a month had passed, she spoke about it.

"What shall we do today?"

"What would you like to do?"

"I knew you were going to ask that. Well, we could do
another drawing."

"We could. Why do you want to do another drawing?"

"You seemed to get so much out of the last ones I did."

"Oh? How so?"

"It made you feel so powerful. You could sit back and
analyze me. Point out all my faults."

"So, you think I got some pleasure out of interpreting your
drawings?"

"Of course. People always get pleasure out of other people's
suffering."

"Who got pleasure out of your suffering? What people are
you talking about?"

"You want me to say 'my mother,' right?"

"Did she do that?"

"Oh, yes. Constantly." She looked up as though slightly
shocked by this admission. "I don't want to talk about my
mother."

"All right. Let's not talk about her."

"Let's talk about the drawings."

"All right."

"Shall we look at the drawings again?"

"All right."

"Would you stop being so agreeable?"

"How would you like me to be?"

"I'd like you to be angry at me."

"What would that do for you?"

"Then . . . then I could also be angry at you without feeling
guilty."

"Yes. And then maybe you could also feel angry at your
mother without feeling guilty."

"Shut up about my mother."

"All right."

"My mother has nothing to do with this!" She glared at him and her eyes became sad and dark. "I don't want to be depressed and angry. I don't want to be withdrawn. I don't want to hate my mother . . . ." She broke into sobs, huddled in her chair like a small, lonesome child, shielding her eyes from the therapist with a self-conscious forearm, as he looked silently on.

Intervention 24

The Rejecting Patient
and the Accepting Therapist

"I've decided to quit therapy," the young man said. He sat forlornly on the chair across from his female therapist. "I just don't think this is working out. And anyway, I don't think I can afford it much longer, because I'm planning to quit my job soon."

The therapist let him talk while she silently came to grips with her separation anxiety and analyzed the situation. He had only been in therapy for a month. She remembered that during the first three sessions he had given her lots of compliments on her appearance and had once jokingly commented that she was "pretty sexy for a shrink." At those times she felt a surge of anxiety. However, when she asked what that meant to him, he would answer, "Nothing," and continue talking of other matters. By the fourth session he was no longer joking and his expression was downcast. The therapist understood that he had apparently wanted more than a therapeutic relationship and had attempted, indirectly, to make that known to her. Having nonverbally refused him, she had made him feel rejected and had rekindled an infantile narcissistic injury.

This was his pattern of relating to people in general and the cause of his retreat into depression and solitude. Knowing he was

too narcissistic for an interpretation and quite unable to verbalize his desires for a nontherapeutic relationship–such desires
having oedipal-incestuous and hence taboo implications–she decided to assist him.

"I feel bad that you want to quit," she said. "I'd miss you if
you didn't come back." The man looked up at her with surprise. "I
must not be giving you what you want," she added. Again he
looked askance at her. "I mean, what would I have to do to keep
you in therapy? If I stopped charging you a fee, would you stay?"
He slowly shook his head. "Then it's not really the money.
Suppose I offered to take you to dinner after each session? Would
that do it?"

His eyes opened wide and a slight smile appeared. "Maybe."

"Well, do you think we ought to talk about that?" She
explained that she was not really inviting him to dinner, but was
interested in exploring thoughts he might be unaware of. He said
he understood, and they began to talk.

By verbalizing for him what he could not verbalize for
himself, she was not only able to keep him in therapy, but also to
focus his attention on his unconscious behavior and begin the
process of analyzing his transference. The intervention was the
antidote to his usual pattern of furtively reaching out and then
retreating into depression. It is an intervention that must be
handled gently and delicately so as not to convey an impression of
leading the patient on, but rather of caring about and wanting to
understand him.

Intervention 25

The Patient Who Broke
a Commitment

Often narcissistic patients will behave in a compliant manner toward their therapists while harboring unconscious resentment against their authority. The resentment, however, gets acted out in various ways.

A pretty young actress was in therapy with an older male therapist. After attending an all-day therapy marathon led by the therapist, she raved about the experience in her next individual session, prompting the therapist to ask if she were interested in joining one of his weekly therapy groups.

"That sounds like a great idea. Is it all right if I start next week?" she replied. She flashed a sweet smile.

"Of course."

When she came in for the following session, she said, "You know, I forgot last week that I'm rehearsing for a play right now, and I'm rehearsing on the night of the group. So, would it be all right if I start the group in three weeks, when this show is over?"

"Sure."

She made no further mention of the group. When three weeks had passed, the therapist brought it up toward the end of the session. "So, will you be at the group on Wednesday night?"

"Well, actually, I meant to tell you." She smiled squeamishly. "I've decided not to join the group. I just don't have the time; I'm always rehearsing on a play or something and it would conflict with my being in a group." Her tone was matter-of-fact, as though she were explaining how to cook rice. "I mean, is it okay?"

"Suppose I said it isn't okay?" the therapist asked. "Do I have a choice?"

"No, I guess not."

The therapist paused a moment to analyze the situation. He felt irritated and understood that this had to do with the fact that the patient had not only broken her commitment but had done so rather blissfully. In her eagerness to please him, she had at first gone along with his suggestion that she join the group; then her resentment about his authority and her fears of what the group might elicit from her had apparently emerged and she had backed out. The therapist pondered whether to simply let the matter drop for now, or to attempt an intervention that might show her how she was acting out feelings and not being responsible to the therapist or to her feelings. She would not be able to handle an interpretation, so he decided to mirror her resistance.

"Since you've changed your mind, would it be all right if I change my mind, too?" he asked, in the same matter-of-fact tone.

"What do you mean?"

"I mean about inviting you to the group."

"I'm not sure what you're saying." Her brow was wrinkled. "Are you saying I can't join the group?"

"That's right."

"But why?"

"You seem to be too busy to make a commitment to the group. Perhaps it would be better to wait until you're ready to make a commitment."

"But that's what I just said." She scratched her hair. "Isn't that what I just said?"

"Is it?"

She fell silent. The therapist had subtly made his point. There were discussions about commitment after that, which in turn led to an exploration of her feelings about institutions and authority figures, her tendency to say "yes" when she meant "no," and her resentment toward her parents and the therapist.

Intervention 26

The Patient Who Wanted Her Therapist to Join Her on the Couch

"Why don't you come over here?" a pretty woman said to her male therapist, patting the couch beside her, smiling coyly.

"What would we do if I came over there?"

"Talk."

"Talk? Why can't we talk like this?"

"It would be more intimate on the couch."

"And what else would we do on the couch?"

"That's all. Just talk."

"Really? What would we talk about?"

"I don't know. Never mind."

The woman had been seductive toward the therapist since starting therapy a few months earlier. She had had affairs with both men and women, and the therapist was aware of her considerable rage at her father, which had become generalized as a rage at men. He knew she was not really interested in him as a person. In fact, she was beset by preoedipal conflicts and was not evolved enough to view men as people who had thoughts and feelings other than those that she projected onto them. She was, in fact, an hysteric with a strong preoedipal substructure, who had been abused by her mother and abandoned by her father as a small child. Her armor consisted of a hard shell of paranoia, which kept everybody, men and women, at a distance. She suspected that everybody was out to abuse her or abandon her, no matter what they said to the contrary. (Had not her father pretended to love her before he abandoned her? Had not her mother continually told her what a good mother she was while putting her down in every way she could?) The therapist might pretend to be a nice man out to help her, but she knew that at bottom he was just another phony like her father, out to seduce and abandon her in the guise of doing therapy. He wanted to get her to trust him, to depend on him, to love him, to revere him as she had once revered her father; and then he would gloat at his power over her. Oh, yes, she knew exactly what he was up to, but she would beat him at his own game.

Up against this kind of wall, the therapist did not know how to intervene. She was blatantly seductive; yet if he tried to analyze or interpret it, she would change the subject or deny the meaning of her behavior. If he said to her, for instance, that she was trying to seduce him, she would say that was his male conceit. Therefore, even though she had now once again attempted in the most obvious way to seduce him, he did not even try to interpret it, for she was sure to use denial once again. Something different, something shocking, was needed in order to jar her out of this pattern.

She had started on another subject when he broke in. "You know, maybe I *should* join you on the couch."

"Oh?" She was surprised. "How come?"

"Maybe it would be helpful to you, therapeutically."

"It would?"

"Sure. We'd be able to talk more intimately, as you put it. Maybe that would be helpful."

"You're just saying that."

"No, I'm serious. Let's talk about it. Maybe it would really be of benefit."

"How would it be of benefit?"

"I'm not sure. What do you think?"

"I'm starting to feel anxious at the pit of my stomach."

"How come?"

"I think if you came over here, if you really came over here and lay on the couch beside me, I'd run out of this room and never come back."

"Then why'd you ask me to lie down beside you?"

"I don't know. I'm getting bored with this subject. Could we talk about something else?"

"Yes, let's talk about something else."

"Fuck you."

"Is that an expression of anger or lust?"

The patient's eyes fell shut and she became drowsy, as often happened when she was angry. For the remainder of the session she went in and out of this twilight state. In the sessions that followed, she claimed not to remember ever having invited the therapist to lie with her on the couch.

However, by joining her resistance and mirroring her se-ductiveness, the therapist had, in essence, driven her anger "above ground." This would have to be repeated again and again before the patient would be ready to acknowledge and analyze her behavior.

Intervention 27

The Fitful Baby
and the Child Therapist

A mother brought her 1-year-old infant to a child therapist. She complained that the child was prone to fits, usually after feeding at the breast. The baby would cry and cry without stopping, four times a day. The mother was beside herself.

The child therapist sat the child on his knee to observe her. She began to cry and tried to bite his knuckle. She cried throughout the consultation.

Three days later the baby was brought back to see the therapist. He again sat the child on his knee. She bit his knuckle several times, almost breaking the skin. He did not retaliate in any way; he just pulled the hand away, gently, and continued to observe the child. She cried and cried and threw stuffed animals on the floor repeatedly.

Two days later the child was brought back for a third time to see the therapist. She again cried and bit the therapist's knuckle severely, without showing any signs of guilt. Again the therapist did not retaliate or even let on that the biting or the crying bothered him. He assumed that the baby was having fits because its mother could not tolerate the baby's aggressive experimentation, which caused the child to get stuck in that stage and in the release of frustration (crying) at the mother's failure to help her get past the stage. In allowing the baby to express her oral-sadistic urges without retaliation, the therapist was able to help her move on to assimilate this experience as another aspect of play. After biting the therapist a few more times and throwing stuffed animals on the floor, the child began fingering her toes outside her shoes. Gradually she stopped crying. The therapist took off her shoes and socks and the child played with her toes, as though trying to pull them off so that she could put them into her mouth. This experiment absorbed her entire interest for about ten minutes.

Four days later the mother returned and said the baby had been "a different child" since the last consultation. She had had no more fits and had slept well at night. The therapist paid a follow-up visit a year later and found that the baby had grown to be a healthy, happy, intelligent, and friendly child. In this case the beginning, middle, and termination phases of treatment were merged together and happened in quick succession.

Intervention 28

The Patient Who Sat in Contorted Positions

One day during the beginning phase, a male patient began describing, with a peculiarly gleeful tone in his voice, how he liked sitting in contorted positions. "I actually prefer sitting with my legs twisted around one another," he told his female therapist. "And sometimes I even sit with my legs around my head. It's *great*. I love it!"

The therapist listened in silence, but took note of the peculiar emphasis he placed on this activity. Later, in an attempt to better understand him, she tried sitting with her own legs twisted around one another, and then made a futile effort to push her legs around the back of her head. While doing so, she began to have a sense of the patient's self-involvement. When he came for his next session, she matter-of-factly acknowledged to him that she had tried putting her legs behind her head, unsuccessfully. "But I noticed something while I was almost in this position," she added. "I realized that if I had been able to put my legs behind my head, that I could then have practically licked my own genitals."

The patient laughed gleefully. "I wasn't going to mention it, but actually, sometimes I do lick myself."

The patient had been keeping the degree of his inversion, his narcissism, and his latent homosexuality from the therapist. It was only because of the therapist's sensitivity to his indirect communication that she was able to understand and come up with the right intervention—exaggeratedly mirroring him—which served to free him from his inhibitions, bring a new closeness between them, and allow for the discussion and analysis of the formerly suppressed material.

Intervention 29

The Shy, Withdrawn Patient

A young woman tended to be socially backward, despite being bright and pretty. Her mother, who prided herself on her beauty and charm, had been unconsciously competitive with the daughter and had thereby turned her into a "shrinking violet." The daughter's female therapist, who she had been seeing for several months, had been working toward making the patient aware of the competitive relationship with her mother, but to no avail.

One day the patient told the therapist she was planning to go to a party that night.

The therapist, pleased with the progress indicated by this decision, replied, "Fine."

During the next session the patient informed the therapist, almost as an afterthought, that she had not gone to the party after all.

"Why?" the therapist asked, surprised.

"Because I didn't think you wanted me to go to the party," the patient replied.

"What made you think that?"

"The way you said, 'Fine'. You said it the same way my

mother used to say it when I'd tell her I was going out with the girls or something. She didn't really mean it, and I didn't think you really meant it."

Through questioning the patient, the therapist had begun the process of bringing to the patient's attention her transference and the ways in which it got acted out.

Intervention 30

The Patient Who Wanted
to Masturbate

He was an odd-looking man who dressed even more oddly than he looked. In his mid-thirties, he had a childlike, cherubic face with pudgy cheeks, pale blue eyes, and hair he had bleached the lightest shade of blond. During the summer in which he had begun therapy with his male therapist he wore mainly knee-length shorts of a loud-colored plaid or polka dot variety, and tank-styled tops that were transparent enough to reveal his hairy chest and the nipples of his somewhat billowy breasts. He had lived in San Francisco, the famous haven for homosexuals, before coming to New York to seek fame and fortune as a rock musician. He was a homosexual with an extreme aversion to being a homosexual; his id impulses drove him toward homosexual life, but his superego viewed this life-style as dirty and evil. Like most homosexuals, he longed for a strong father figure who would forgive him his "indiscretions" with his mother (he had had a close-bonded, flirtatious relationship with her), help him to separate from her, help him come to grips with his fear of the archaic witch-mother, and accept him as a man.

His way of attempting to bring all of this about with respect to his therapist was to talk again and again about masturbation.

Because of his conflicts, he had no sex life at all other than that of masturbation. He loathed himself for going out with men, but feared and had contempt for women. So he masturbated, and felt guilty about that as well.

"I masturbated again last night," he would tell his therapist. "As usual, I wasn't able to come. I kept getting distracted. If I started fantasizing about doing it with a man, I'd get turned off. Then I'd try to think about a woman, like you suggested, but that didn't work either. What happened was I started thinking about my mother. I started thinking about how, when I was a kid, I'd have to come home from school and brush my mother's hair. All the other kids would go outside and play, but not me. I had to brush my mother's hair for hours and hours. I had to stand on this little stool so I could reach her head. She'd sit in front of her dresser. I can still remember vividly how the top of her head looked. There was a mole right in the center. I hated that mole. I hated her, but I couldn't say anything. And she would always say to me, 'Promise me you'll never leave me, promise me.' That's what I kept thinking about while I was masturbating. What do you make of that, Doc?"

"What do *you* make of it?"

"I knew you were going to ask that. I don't know. I don't know what to make of it. You're the Doc."

"Yes, I'm the Doc. But it's more important that you discover things for yourself."

"That's what you keep telling me."

The patient lay on the couch, his hands clasped and resting on his slightly rotund belly, his eyes emotionless. The therapist knew he was frustrated because the therapist was not providing him with ready answers to his problems. On a deeper level, he was frustrated because the therapist was not responding to his seduction. What he really wanted was for the therapist to take him, anally, and thereby initiate him into the world of manhood. This act would be a way of symbolically appeasing his father and gaining forgiveness and acceptance as a fellow man among men.

However, as the therapist well knew, this form of initiation into manhood could only be illusory; for if the therapist were to act it out the patient would only feel all the more confused and all the more inadequate as a man. It would simply be an enactment of the negative oedipal impulses that had first arisen in the patient in early childhood as a response to a pathological familial environment. "What are you thinking?" the therapist asked the patient after a while.

"I was thinking about masturbating."

"What about it?"

"I was thinking I'd like to masturbate right now." The patient always spoke in a matter-of-fact tone of voice, displaying a dissociated, borderline substructure to his character.

"What would that do for you?"

"I'm not sure. I think it would help me in some way."

"But how?"

"I don't know. Forget it."

"Are you angry?"

"No. I'm just tired of answering all your questions."

This was not the first time the patient had expressed the desire to masturbate during a session. The therapist had tried different interventions to deal with this peculiar form of resistance. He had asked the patient to have a fantasy that he was masturbating; the patient had been unable and unwilling to do so. He had tried to interpret that the patient's desire to masturbate in front of him was an attempt to gain his father's acceptance of his masculine strivings; the patient had listened to and parroted the interpretation, but he forgot it by the next session. The therapist tried a paradoxical joining of the resistance: "Maybe we should forget about therapy and go down to your apartment and masturbate together." The patient had taken the therapist up on his offer. "What do you think would happen if we masturbated together? Where would it lead?" the therapist asked. The patient had replied, smiling brightly, that hopefully it would lead to a mutual orgasm.

Now the patient had again brought up masturbating in the office, and the therapist was getting a bit perturbed. The patient's refusal to free-associate and his adamant insistence upon masturbating in the office were not just a symbolic acting-out of negative oedipal impulses, but also an act of spite and an expression of narcissistic rage. This rage was arousing a masochistic countertransference reaction in the therapist, who had begun to view the patient as a tormentor (as his little brother had been), one whom he needed to tame or get rid of. However, after analyzing this countertransference, he was able to neutralize his feelings of frustration and anger and use them to understand the patient. What he understood was that the patient's demand to masturbate was a disguised threat. "Let me masturbate, or I'll leave therapy." Unconsciously, the patient wanted either to drive the therapist into kicking him out of therapy, or to provide himself with a justification for leaving therapy, so he would not have to deal with his underlying conflicts.

"Suppose I don't allow you to masturbate?" the therapist asked. "Suppose you keep coming in each week, wanting to masturbate, and I never allow you to do it. Then what?"

"I don't know," the patient said, gazing blankly at the wall.

"Will you quit and find another therapist who'll let you masturbate?"

"I might."

"Well, then I suppose you'll be quitting soon."

"Why?"

"Because I'll never allow you to masturbate here."

"Why not?"

"Because it would be extremely detrimental to your therapy, not to mention unethical. You need to deal with the feelings underneath your desire to masturbate. That's what will be helpful to you."

"You think I'm angry at you?"

"Yes, I do."

The patient paused, and something flickered in his eyes.

"Maybe I am a little angry. And a little jealous, too. I think you feel superior to me because you're straight and you're a big-shot analyst."

"Just a *little* angry?"

"Maybe more than a little."

"Tell me about it," the therapist said. He had confronted the patient's disguised threat and had finally gotten him to acknowledge and talk about his feelings. The patient did not bring up masturbating in the office again.

Intervention 31

The Noninterpretation of Dreams

A man told his male therapist about a dream. It was a complex dream, the symbolism of which was rather obscure—a type of dream common to those suffering from a severe form of narcissism, fixated in pregenitality. When he was finished telling the dream, he asked the therapist, "So what do you think?"

"What do *you* think?" the therapist replied.

"It doesn't matter what I think. I'm paying you for *your* opinion."

"I don't think it would be beneficial to you to hear what I think."

"Why not?"

"Because you need to understand things for yourself, at your own pace. My telling you what the dream means to me isn't going to help you do that."

"I see." With that the man proceeded to provide his own associations to the dream.

The therapist refused to interpret this man's dream, even though he solicited an interpretation, because he knew that in the early stages of therapy narcissistic patients do not respond well to interpretation of any kind. He knew also that this particular patient had paranoid features to his personality and that his request for an interpretation was a trap. What he really wanted was to challenge the therapist's interpretation and defeat him. Since a therapeutic alliance had not yet been formed, the therapist was still viewed by the patient as a threatening preoedipal parent figure. By not interpreting the dream, the therapist stayed out of the trap and provided, instead, a facilitating environment.

Intervention 32

The Patient Who Came Late

Early in therapy a young woman walked into the therapist's office a few minutes late and breathlessly explained, "I couldn't find a parking place."

She lay on the couch, sighing and flopping her legs down in a gesture of exhaustion. Her therapist, a man a little older than her, noted this bit of resistance but decided not to make an issue of it. To point this out to her right then as a form of resistance might have been a mistake, since it was not yet clear that she was resisting. Furthermore, even if it was a resistance, she was still too defensive at that moment to be able to hear such an interpretation. He waited in silence, hoping for more "evidence."

During the course of the session the patient fell silent several times. Toward the end of the hour she said, "Oh, by the way, I did have a dream last night, but I forgot it as soon as I woke up."

The therapist's silence had facilitated the growth of her resistance throughout the session. Upon her admission of forgetting her dream, the therapist felt he had enough evidence to pin her down.

"You seem to be avoiding something," he told her. "You

came a bit late, then you had several lapses of silence, and now you tell me you've forgotten your dream."

"Just because I came late and forgot my dream you think I'm avoiding something?" The patient was still not entirely ready to open up. "I think that's a bit ridiculous."

The therapist fell silent again. To pursue an interpretation that a patient defends against is futile. He waited for her to speak.

"Well, actually, now that I think of it, I did feel upset when I left you after last session."

Intervention 33

The Militant Lesbian
and the Heterosexual Therapist

"The reason I came to you," she said, glancing proprietarially around the room, "was because you work with artists. I'm a sculptress, and my art is practically my whole life. Well, it's one of two things that are important to me. One is art. The other is my lesbianism. I'm a politically active lesbian." She looked at the therapist pointedly.

The therapist smiled and nodded noncommittally.

"I think one reason I've never gone into therapy before is because I never felt a therapist could really understand me. Maybe I had a stereotypical attitude toward therapists. I saw them all as conservative, rigid types. I didn't think they'd understand me the way I want to be understood." She glared at the therapist again. She was a middle-aged woman in jeans and a T-shirt, with short-cropped hair combed in a pompadour. She sat with her legs spread out, the way some men sit when they want to reveal their genitals to a woman. "I like your place," she said, looking around again. "Did you do any of the paintings in here?"

"No. They were all done by patients."

"I see. You call them 'patients'? That's interesting. Do you paint? It says in your brochure you paint. But you say none of these are yours? I'm glad you're a painter, though. That makes me feel you'll understand me. Yes, I feel comfortable in this space." She sat sensuously back on the couch, her arms stretched out to each side and resting on the floral-patterned cushions. "It's very important to me to be understood on *my* terms," she continued. "God knows my family never did. They always regarded me as an oddball. I think most people regard artists as oddballs, don't you? I remember meeting a woman once at a party. I think she was on the make for me, and she leaned forward, you know?" The patient herself leaned forward, toward the therapist, a seductive glimmer in her eyes. "She smiled at me and she said, 'Is it true that all artists are crazy?' And I said to her in an absolutely straight way—and believe me, I can be as absolutely straight as I want to be, that's one of the things people don't understand about me, but that's another matter—anyway, I looked at her and said, 'How crazy would you like me to be?' That shut her up."

The patient continued to ramble in this seductive and provocative manner and the therapist listened in silence. The therapist was opposite in just about every way from the patient. While the patient was a macho type, the therapist was a traditionally feminine woman, also of about middle age, clad in a long, flowery dress, wearing make-up and jewelry, and with long hair tied neatly in a bun. Because of the way the patient was sitting, the therapist found herself looking at the patient's crotch. Sexual feelings welled up in her, mixed with annoyance. She studied these feelings and realized that the patient was being both provocative and frustrating; provocative in her nonverbal communication and frustrating in that she would ask questions but not really be interested in an answer, not really letting the therapist get a word in. The therapist knew that this was probably how someone in the patient's family had communicated with her and that now this form of communication was being passed on to the therapist. Since this was the initial interview, the therapist chose not to say anything. She knew that if she was silent long enough the patient would give her an opening.

When it came, the opening was not quite the kind the therapist might have hoped for. The patient had finished a story involving her homosexuality. Suddenly she turned to the therapist, leaned forward again challengingly, and asked, "So tell me, how do you feel about homosexuality?" A bitter smile glared from her eyes.

"That's a rather broad question," the therapist replied, taken aback. "What do you mean?"

"You *know* what I mean."

"No, I don't know what you mean."

"Let me put it this way." The patient chuckled contemptuously, as though she had just pinned an enemy to the ground. "Do you think homosexuality is a perversion? A disease? Unnatural? Abnormal?" She smiled with all her teeth.

The therapist felt trapped. Her immediate response was of indignation at being so trapped, along with an impulse to dismiss her. She had encountered other militant homosexuals, both male and female, and had become familiar with their contempt for heterosexuals. They seemed to have a need to prove that all heterosexuals were "bad"—they were all homophobics or bigots or reactionaries—and to show that homosexuals were superior to heterosexuals. They seemed to want everybody to be homosexual, never stopping to consider how the human race could survive if that were the case. The therapist understood that their need to prove themselves superior stemmed from their narcissism, and that their rage against heterosexuals was a generalized transference of oedipal and preoedipal frustrations. After a minute or two she came to grips with the feelings the patient had aroused.

"Instead of answering your question, I'd like to ask you one," she said. "Why are you looking at me that way? What's that smile about? Why were you chuckling before?" Her voice was so low it was almost a whisper. "What are you feeling about me?" She had decided to call attention to the patient's feelings rather than to the content of what she was saying, hoping to demonstrate to her the transferential nature of those feelings, which harkened back to the family that had always regarded her as an oddball.

The patient smiled gleefully at the therapist. "I don't feel anything about you."

The therapist mirrored the patient, smiling gleefully back at her. "That's what I thought."

The patient stopped smiling. "What's that supposed to mean?"

"You're *acting* as if you don't feel anything about me. As if I'm not even human."

"So?"

"So, I wonder whether it matters to you one way or another what my views are about homosexuality?"

"Probably not."

"Then why ask?"

"I guess I just wanted to see if you'd be honest."

"And if I were honest, what would I say?"

"That you think homosexuality is a disease."

"And if I said it wasn't?"

"I wouldn't believe you."

"Then I'm out either way?"

"Seems so."

"So where do we go from here?"

"I don't know."

The patient decided to come back for another session, but she ended up quitting after a few weeks anyway. However, the therapist's interventions in the initial interview did succeed in putting a slight crack in her narcissistic defense. Sometimes that is the best that one can do.

Intervention 34

The Patient Who Felt Hopeless

"I feel hopeless," the slightly graying man told his therapist again and again.

"You keep saying that," the therapist replied.

"Because it's true."

"Are you trying to convince me that you're hopeless?"

"Maybe I am."

For several months the therapy had been stagnating. The patient, a law student, did not think he could make it through school. He had already dropped out once before and was on the verge of doing so again. He also felt hopeless with respect to women and with respect to dealing with his mother's continual interference in his life. The therapist, a man of around the same age as the patient, found himself feeling hopeless as well. However, on this day, as the patient lay on the couch muttering about his hopelessness, the therapist decided to investigate the patient's feelings more completely. The patient's hopelessness was his usual mode of defense, one that had come into play in all aspects of his life; so it was only natural that it would come into play in therapy as well, after the initial "honeymoon" period was over.

"Why would you want to convince me that you're hopeless?" the therapist pursued.

"Maybe you'll agree and kick me out of therapy."

"And then what? How will that solve your problems?"

"Then I won't have to think about how hopeless I am."

"How will that help you?"

"I don't know. Maybe if I keep telling you how hopeless I feel you'll be able to understand me."

"What will I understand?"

"That I'm hopeless."

"How will that help you?"

"I don't know."

The patient lapsed into silence. The therapist waited a respectable period of time and then offered an explanation.

"You see, understanding your hopelessness isn't going to help you get better. What will help you get better is dealing with your resistance to talking out your thoughts, feelings, and memories as they occur to you—dealing with your blocks to free association. When we can understand and deal with those blocks, we will have solved all the rest of your problems as well. They're all interrelated."

"You think my hopelessness is a form of resistance?"

"That's right."

The patient and the therapist continued to talk about the patient's resistance via hopelessness. They had many arguments about this notion, which led to the patient getting in touch with the repressed anger beneath the feeling of hopelessness—a rage at his mother, his father, and his grandmother, who had all contributed to his chronic feeling of low self-esteem.

Intervention 35

The Therapist Who Told a Story

A therapist was having a difficult time with a female patient who was acting out her resistance in ways that were destructive to her treatment. He had put her into his therapy group only to have her quit a few months later. Then she decided to join the group again, but at the last minute she changed her mind and did not show up. The same thing happened once more.

"I'm afraid I will not be able to consider any further requests of yours to join the group," he told her during her next individual session.

"Why?"

"Because you're obviously resistant to the group, and you're acting out that resistance in ways that are destructive to the group."

"How am I being destructive to the group?"

"First of all, you quit the group suddenly one night without discussing it with me or the group. Then you've asked to join the group several times since then, and each time you've changed your mind and not shown up at the appointed group."

"I didn't mean anything against you or the group," the patient protested. "I think you're taking this personally. I'm just having a hard time making up my mind, that's all. I don't know why you say that's destructive. How's that destructive?"

The therapist debated the issue with her briefly and then decided such a debate would get them nowhere. "I'll tell you what," he said in a different voice—a voice a parent uses with a small child. "I just thought of a good story. You like stories, don't you? Would you care to hear this story?"

"Go ahead," the patient warily replied.

"Oh, good. Once there was this man and woman. They met at a party. They seemed to like each other and the man asked the woman for her phone number. The next week he called her up."

"Is the woman me?" the patient asked.

"Does she sound like you?"

"Never mind. Go on."

"So the man called up the woman and asked her to go to a movie with him that Saturday night. Some intriguing foreign film in the Village. You like foreign films, don't you? So did this woman, and she accepted. But when Saturday night rolled around, he didn't show up."

"I think I know this story."

"Yes, it *does* have a familiar ring to it, doesn't it? So anyway, the man didn't show up and the woman called him and asked what happened. He said he was sorry but he was just feeling ambivalent about women these days and he had changed his mind. He hoped she wouldn't take it personally, because it didn't have anything to do with her. It was just his ambivalence about women. She said she understood, and they made plans to go out the following week. However, guess what happened the following week?"

"I have no idea."

"The man didn't show up again. Now what do you think of this story? Should the woman have been angry at him, or do you think he was just being ambivalent and she should have understood his feelings?"

"It's not the same thing as happened with the group."

"How so?"

"Because it was personal. It was between two people. When I didn't show up for the group, that was between me and a thing— the group. Or between me and a professional—my therapist. I'm paying you so I can be in therapy with you, so why should I have to think about your feelings?"

"Oh, I see. Because I'm a professional you don't have to be concerned about my feelings or the group's. What are we, automatons?"

Several sessions later the patient brought it up as an aside. "Oh, by the way, could you write down that story you told me the other day? I was trying to tell it to a friend, and I couldn't remember it exactly." She laughed. "My friend thought it was funny that I thought of you as an automaton. But I guess I did. I really did."

Intervention 36

The Patient Who Could Not Say No To His Father

A young man complained to his therapist that his father wanted him to work for him at his hardware store. Ever since the patient had been a child, his father had spoken of the day when he would take over his business. "I don't know how to tell him that I don't want to do it," the patient said. "It will break his heart if I tell him." For several months the patient's sessions were centered on his inability to talk to his father.

"Perhaps I could talk to your father for you," the therapist finally offered. The therapist made the offer knowing that, because of the nature of his character, the patient could not possibly accept it. There was a part of him that wanted the therapist to do just that—speak to his father for him. Indeed, his mother had played that role up to now, but in this instance she sided with the father. There was another part of the patient that would have felt demeaned if the therapist actually did talk to his father. An interpretation would have had little effect, as the patient was quite narcissistic and during his three years of therapy he had continually demonstrated a lack of tolerance for such interventions. By actually making the offer, the therapist was allowing the patient to experience his unconscious conflicts with respect to dependence and independence and to understand how it was being played out in the transference. After they had discussed the pros and cons of the therapist's speaking to the father on the patient's behalf, the patient realized he was trying to get the therapist to take his mother's role.

"I have to do this myself," he said. "It's time I grew up."

Intervention 37

The Embarrassed Patient and the Therapist Who Sought Elaboration

She spoke often of her sexual longings for her therapist, a handsome man in his mid-forties, but she was embarrassed as she did so, blushing and sighing and lapsing into silence. She spoke of walking on the street and having a flash of him holding her in his arms; of reading a book and seeing the two of them as hero and heroine; of calling out to him at night before she went to sleep. But she was married and it was not right for her to have such feelings for her therapist, she told him, and she could not say more. All during the first few months of her therapy she was consumed by these feelings but could not do much more than sketch them. They were embarrassing, she told him, very embarrassing.

The therapist realized that the picture was not getting deeper or clearer. However, there seemed to be a good working alliance, so he asked her to elaborate on her sexual feelings in order to shed light on the transference. "You seem to be full of sexual feelings for me, but you haven't really given me a clear picture of what you imagine about us." He spoke in neither a crude nor a timid way. "What are your fantasies about me?"

The patient began in a halting voice. "I guess . . . I'd want you to take me into your arms, squeeze me so tight I could hardly breathe . . . and then lift me off the ground and carry me to bed." She paused and the therapist asked her to go on. "This is embarrassing, but if you think it's important. . . . Well, you'd sort of tear off my nightgown and kiss my mouth hard—so hard it hurts and I can hardly breathe. Then you'd . . . ram your penis into me. It would be very large and it would hurt, but I'd like it." She fell silent for a moment. "And, also, I imagine you—I don't know if this is important—I imagine you as being unshaven in this fantasy, and your beard scratches my face."

The therapist analyzed the fantasy in silence. There were two references to being unable to breathe, reminding him that the patient had had asthma at around the age of 6, when her mother married an abusive stepfather. There were also references to being lifted off the ground, carried, and to the therapist's large penis. "What do you make of my being unshaven?" the therapist asked. "Did anybody use to scratch you with his beard?"

"My stepfather," the patient blurted out. "He used to love to torment me by rubbing his face against mine. And he'd grab me and squeeze me until I could hardly breathe and throw me into the air . . . ."

Intervention 38

The Therapist Who Charged
for a Missed Appointment

A young man lay silently on the couch.

"What are you thinking?" the therapist asked.

"I'm thinking that I'm annoyed at you."

"What for?"

"For charging me for that session I missed two weeks ago."

"Do you really mean that you're annoyed? You sound angry."

"I guess maybe I'm a little angry."

"Just a little," the therapist prodded.

With that the patient suddenly exploded into a rage. "If you want to know the truth, I think you're a hypocrite. You pretend you're a Good Samaritan, this person who cares about people, but you're really just out for the money, just another tight-assed old man, like my father. But you hide your hypocrisy behind all that psychoanalytic crap. Someday maybe I'll rub your nose in your own crap. I'll do to you what you do to me."

"What do I do to you?"

"You make me grovel through all my shit, and you never let up. You're never satisfied; perform or get out. It's never enough."

The therapist, through maintaining firm boundaries

(charging for the missed session), and through the intervention of investigative prodding, was able to uncover—behind the innocent annoyance about the fee—the anal-sadistic fury and humiliation of this patient's childhood. Sometimes the most ordinary of circumstances, when explored, can lead to a therapeutic breakthrough.

Intervention 39

The Patient Who Wanted to Be Kicked Out of Therapy

Throughout the early phase of therapy, a somewhat overweight and withholding young woman would taunt her male therapist with statements such as, "I'll bet you're getting bored with me," and "I could never do your job. I'd want to kill all my patients," and "I'll bet you feel like kicking me out of therapy." She was a woman who had had a series of destructive relationships, beginning with her father and younger brother and culminating with several love relationships in which she had actually so enraged the men involved that they would figuratively kick her out of their lives. However, the patient was in touch only with her depression and denied any feelings of anger, particularly toward the therapist. Whenever he would attempt to analyze her statements, she would tease him, saying, "Look, if you want me to say I'm angry at you, then I'll say it. But I don't really feel it."

One day she spent most of the session making flippant comments and attempting to engage the therapist in banter. Eventually she got around to telling him, once again, that she guessed he must feel like killing her or kicking her out of therapy.

"Quite frankly," he answered, "I do have those feelings right now. I feel like kicking you out of therapy." The therapist had sensed that the way to break down her denial was through an emotional rather than an intellectual communication. She was an intellectual, skilled at verbal play, and well defended against any kind of analytical questions or comments. "In fact," he added, "it might give me a great deal of satisfaction to kick you out."

The patient lay very still. "You're not just saying that?"

"No, I mean it. I really feel that way. I thought you should know what kind of feelings you're arousing, since you asked." The therapist spoke in a matter-of-fact manner, without any rancor. "You seem to be able to express anger only by acting it out, rather than by verbalizing it," he added.

The patient thought about it for a while, then admitted, "I guess I *am* angry at you. It makes me angry that I have to pay you to come here and do this. I don't even want to be here in the first place, and then to have to pay you as well . . . ."

Intervention 40

Catching Patients
Is Like Catching Fish

A novice therapist had a tendency to lose patients early in treatment. They would come to him for several months, sometimes even for a year or so, and then quit. Usually they would discuss with him why they felt like quitting. Often they would say they did not have the money. His approach would be to tell them they could quit if they wanted to but that he felt they still had problems to work out and that they might be acting out their resistance by quitting. This approach seldom worked, and most quit anyway, leaving the therapist feeling rejected and hurt. He put the problem to his supervisor.

The supervisor was somewhat of a jokester. He would advise the therapist using the accent and character of Charlie Chan from the mystery movies of olden days. "Well, my son, you have not understood the problem," he would say, sitting back knowingly in his chair. "You see, catching patients is like catching fish. Patients come to you and in the beginning they nibble enthusiastically at your bait (psychoanalysis)—but they don't really take the big bite. They nibble and they nibble and you wait with your rod and reel in your hand. A month passes. Two months. Three months. A year. You wait, my son, you wait. And then one day it happens. The fish takes a bite, and no sooner does he take it than he runs. Now, depending on what kind of fish he is, you must either give him a lot of slack or tug sharply on your line. It is the same thing with your patients. Your patients, they come and they take the big bite—they get in touch with something—and they want to run. When that happens, what do *you* do? Always the same thing, whether they are big fish who need a lot of slack, or little fish who need a sharp tug, always you react the same way. You try to hold on to them. You are so afraid to lose them that you try to hold on to them. You do not give them slack and you do not give them a sharp tug and then let them be. You just hold on. That is wrong, my son, wrong."

"What is the right way, O Master?"

"A very good question, my son. Very, very good question. Let us say it is a big fish. This kind of fish is very stubborn and very strong, and if you try to hold on to him he will break your line. You must let him run until he gets tired. In other words, we're talking here about those grandiose personalities who will run even harder when anybody attempts to control them. They must be given a lot of slack. They want to take three vacations? Let them. They want to take a six-month leave of absence? Let them. They will be back. They are leaving to test the therapist to see if he or she will try to control them. So you let them run and run and run and then, at long last, they exhaust themselves and settle in. When they get settled in you can finally pull on the line and they will no longer mind. Then you can guide them, pull them in your boat toward the deeper waters. Do you understand about the big fish, my son?"

"Yes, O Master. But what of the little fish?"

"Another excellent question, my son. Now, with the little fish you must give them a sharp tug when they start to run, because they are very tricky and if you do not be careful they will get away and never come back. These are the guilt-ridden personalities, the frightened people, the self-defeatists. For example, if they tell you they may have to leave therapy because they are running out of money, you must immediately tug on the line. You may tell them that if they do not get the money you may have to terminate them. Or you may tell them that if they quit therapy in an irresponsible way, you may not be available for them again. Or you may give them a lecture about commitment. But however, you must act quickly, before they start their run. Once they have begun their run it is difficult to stop them any longer. That is another mistake you make, my son; you try to stop them after they have begun their run. What I am saying is that you give them a negative stimulus the moment they mention leaving, so that you thereby condition them to stay. This is only a temporary conditioning, of course, to be reversed when they have completed their therapeutic work. Do you understand, my son?"

"Yes. Give them a sharp tug."

"Very good. Very, very good. And most of all, the timing has to be right. You must give slack or pull on the line at exactly the right time, otherwise you may lose the fish. And don't be afraid of hurting the fish's (I mean, the patient's) feelings. Deep down, they really want to be hooked by you. It makes them feel comfortable. And once that hook is in their little mouths – or big mouths – they have become patients in the truest sense. That is when the analysis really begins. Do you understand what I'm saying, Number One Son?"

"I think so," the therapist replied, nodding emphatically.

"You think so?" The supervisor raised a bushy eyebrow. "So what will you do the next time a patient talks about leaving therapy?"

"Give him slack or a sharp tug."

"And then?"

"Analyze him."

"May the Buddha look with kindness on you."

PART TWO

INTERVENTIONS OF THE MIDDLE PHASE

Intervention 41

Breaking Through to the Middle Phase

Quite often the middle phase of therapy begins with the first big breakthrough—that first instance when a patient gets in touch with a warded-off feeling or thought and understands with his whole being that, yes, there is an unconscious. The feeling or thought may concern the therapist, the patient's parents, or other primary figures in his life. It may be accompanied by a memory and may lead to a new insight. This breakthrough signals the beginning of the working-through process—that laborious job of going over and over the traumatic material until the patient is rid of its influence on his life, including its ramifications in the transference.

Typical of such breakthroughs was that of a young man who had been in therapy with a male therapist for about four years without shedding a tear. A borderline schizoid character with a passive-aggressive substructure, his relationships with women and with his therapist were exercises in "guerilla warfare." He had had an abusive mother who treated him and his siblings (he being the oldest) as though they were privates and she the commanding officer of an army platoon. Meanwhile his father was a passive type who drank to excess and was eventually driven by the mother's tyranny to a nervous breakdown and had to be hospitalized. This episode had been quite traumatic to the patient. He had needed a father who would rescue him from this tyrannical mother and initiate him into the world of manhood; instead his father had been defeated by her and retreated into the mental wards. Subsequently the patient had developed a defense mechanism of passive aggression toward everybody, the aim of which was to gain revenge against his mother. He invariably became involved with women very much like his mother, dominating and controlling women who saw in him an apparently docile individual they could control and mold into their own image; how mistaken they were! Through his "guerrilla warfare" techniques—which consisted primarily of a docile, loving subterfuge that hid a sneaky, subtly rejecting backlash—he always ended up driving them into a rage and they would then kick him out of their lives in a fury. He did not mind this, since he knew he had driven them to it.

The same pattern repeated itself in the transference. The patient related to the therapist in a submissive manner, presenting the persona of a sensitive, earnest, caring young man who wanted very much to please his therapist. If the therapist made an interpretation about his passive aggression, for example, the patient would dutifully and earnestly repeat the interpretation several times and make it a point to bring it up during the next session or two. However, this was all a pretense, for underneath he regarded the therapist as an adversary, a potential tyrant like his mother whom he must appease and keep at bay and at some point defeat. Just when the therapist began to believe he was making some progress, the patient would disappear, literally or figuratively. Once he announced he was leaving therapy to go to a Zen monastery. On another occasion he suddenly took a series of freelance photography assignments that required him to travel to foreign lands, again interrupting the therapy, much to the therapist's chagrin.

"You seem to continually want to run from me," the therapist would say to him when he returned.

"Yes, yes," the patient would earnestly reply. "That's true. People are always telling me that. I do that, I know. I don't understand it myself."

"How do you feel about me?"

"I think you're a nice guy. I admire you."

"Then why do you run from me?"

"I suppose I'm afraid of you."

"You suppose?"

"All right. I *am* afraid of you."

"But do you feel that?"

"No, not really."

He was almost completely out of touch with his feelings. For four years the therapist had struggled with the patient until, finally, the breakthrough occurred during a group therapy marathon. The therapist had the patient sit face-to-face with a pretty young woman for whom he had expressed affection. Having noticed that he had difficulty looking into the woman's eyes, the therapist asked the patient to try to keep his gaze fastened onto her. "Look at her eyes," he said.

"It's hard," the patient said, looking at the therapist.

"I know. That's why I want you to keep doing it. Come on. Look at her. Look in her eyes and tell her what you feel when you look in her eyes."

The patient laughed embarrassedly and at first could express only his positive, superficial feelings. "I feel you're . . . a pretty girl . . . and I like you. I feel good about you."

"Do you have any negative feelings?" the therapist asked.

"Not that I'm aware of." The patient kept looking away from her eyes.

"Keep looking at her."

"I'm trying."

"I'd like you to repeat what I'm going to say now," the

therapist said. "Say, 'I'm afraid of you.' Look at her and say that: 'I'm afraid of you.' " He was using a Gestalt therapy intervention.

"That's hard. That's really hard." The patient kept looking away.

"Say it."

The patient looked at the young woman, who returned his gaze noncommittally.

"I'm . . . I'm afraid of you."

" 'And down deep I hate you,' " the therapist interspersed. "Say that to her."

"But I don't hate her."

"Say it anyway. See what it feels like to say it."

"And deep down . . . I hate you." The patient said it but could not look into her eyes; he looked at her mouth, at her ears, at her neck, anywhere but her eyes.

"Look at her," the therapist said. "Look at her and say, 'Deep down I hate you and I'll die before I let you control me!' "

The patient repeated this sentence and seemed to have a great deal of difficulty remembering it. When he remembered it he could not say it while looking into the woman's eyes. It took about ten minutes before he could do it. Then his entire body began to shake with the aggression that had been pent up within him for so many years, and there was a look of wonderment in his eyes as well as of rage. He kept repeating the phrase, "And I'll die before I'll let you control me!"—no longer needing the therapist's prompting. Yes, that was where he was stuck. The phrase took hold of him and became an obsessive ritual; those were his core feelings, the ones he had been acting out for years without being aware of it. Again and again he said it until the shaking became a sobbing and he fell into her arms to cry with his child's heart at long last. The middle phase had begun with a fanfare, and now there would be several more years of working through.

Intervention 42

Working Through

Again and again a female patient in her middle thirties recalled a particular childhood memory. At the age of four she had found after masturbating somewhat obsessively that her vagina had begun to bleed. She ran to her father in a panic. He looked up from his newpaper and said, "It's nothing. It will go away. Just forget about it." He went back to his paper. Each time the memory came up, her therapist, a gentle older man, would attempt to understand it. In the beginning of this working-through process, the analysis concentrated on her feelings of rejection, on her penis envy, on her feelings of inadequacy as a woman, and on her desire to take her mother's place in her father's eyes.

Then at a later point in the analysis the woman developed a resistance to coming to her sessions. She began to talk of being afraid of the therapist. "There's something ominous about you that scares me," she told him.

The therapist asked for a clarification. "What is it about me that scares you?"

"I'm not sure."

"Do you want to be sure?"

"Maybe not."

"Why not?"

"Maybe I'm afraid to hurt your feelings." She paused. "But that's absurd. Why should I be concerned about your feelings? I'm paying you to be able to say these things to you." She paused again. "Actually, I think you're too passive. Your silence scares me. That's it. I mean, you act friendly and caring on the surface, but I think that you're secretly hostile to women. And that hostility comes out in your passivity. I can't stand your passivity. I'll bet that if one of your female patients was bleeding to death you would just let her bleed. You'd sit there silently letting her bleed to death." Suddenly the patient caught herself. "Oh, my God! I know what that is—my father . . . ." Once again she recalled the memory of bleeding from her vagina. Only this time, for the first time, she became aware of the hidden sadistic qualities in her supposedly kindly father's passivity.

Intervention 43

The Therapist Who Had No Ears

A woman patient found herself feeling bored with her therapy and convinced she was not making any progress. When her therapist, a classical psychoanalyst, asked why she was bored and felt she was not making progress, the patient could not say.

"I don't know exactly why. Maybe I've worked out everything I wanted to work out in therapy. I felt I was making some progress the first two years, but it seems as though for the last year or so nothing has been happening. When I come here I have nothing to say."

"How are you feeling about me?" asked the therapist, a young woman still in training.

"I like you," the patient replied.

The therapist sensed that there were some negative feelings the patient was unable to verbalize. In the three years she had been seeing this woman, the therapist had encountered several similar periods during which the patient had complained of boredom and of not making progress. However, in the past, these periods had lasted only a short time, and they seemed to have been overcome simply by the patient's being able to speak about them. The therapist did not know how to intervene. She discussed the case with her supervisor, who noted that the patient was a graphic designer. "Have her draw a picture of you," the supervisor suggested. "Perhaps she'll be able to visualize what she can't verbalize."

When they next met, the therapist gave the patient an assignment to draw a picture of her. "Don't try to make it artistic," the therapist said. "Just try to express your feelings about me."

"I'll try," the patient replied hesitantly.

She returned the following week with a full-blown portrait of the therapist, done in rich charcoal. It was one of those flattering portraits, such as those done by street artists; it made the therapist look like a movie star. However, there was one significant detail missing.

"Where are my ears?" the therapist asked, looking at the drawing.

"Oh, my God!" the patient said, covering her open mouth with her hand.

"So," the therapist said, putting the drawing down and sitting back in her chair, "do you want to tell me what you think I don't listen to?"

The patient smirked like a schoolgirl and began to explain for the first time how she did not feel listened to or understood by the therapist, and also, long before that, by her mother.

Intervention 44

Artistic Sensitivity and Neurotic Sensitivity

He was an intense young man in his late twenties who harbored a particular notion about artists. "To be an artist, you have to suffer," he would say again and again. "It comes with the territory." He had been in therapy for several years and had spent much of that time explaining in vivid detail the many ways he suffered as an artist. "You don't know what it's like in the music world," he would explain in a voice tinged with resignation. "They treat you like an animal. There's so much pettiness, so much manipulation, so much vanity. I'd like to just do my music and not have to worry about the politics, but if you want to get ahead you've got to make contacts." What riled him most was that other people were better at making contacts. "I found out today that George Bollinger got a fifty-thousand-dollar deal from Atlantic," he would moan. "I used to jam with him and he's nothing more than a poseur."

Several times a month his mother would call him and tell him how well his younger brother was doing in medical school. His mother had been telling him how well his younger brother was doing ever since he had been born, four years after him. She had told him how well his younger brother had first walked and how nicely he went to the potty. ("You didn't go to the potty until you were two-and-a-half," she reminded him.) Later, in grade school, she crooned over how popular the little brother was and in high school how he excelled in sports and made the honor roll. ("You never made the honor roll," she told him from time to time.) In despair he retreated to his own world, a world filled with music—his one great love. Now, as a young adult, he still heard from his mother about how well his younger brother was doing; yet he seldom spoke of his mother or his younger brother during his psychotherapy sessions.

"I wish I could explain to you how it is in the New York music scene," he would say. "I mean, I know my music is good. I know it's good. If there's one thing I know, it's that my work is good. But that's not enough. You need to be a politician. Like George Bollinger and all the rest of the no-talent jerks." He looked at the therapist with his dark, brooding eyes.

"And your younger brother?" the therapist, an older man, interspersed.

"What about him?"

"Is he a politician?"

He laughed bitterly. "Funny you should mention him. Yes, the ultimate politician. He could always get anything he wanted from my mother. Anything. But I don't want to talk about him. That's all in the past. I don't care about my little brother. What really ticks me off are the no-talent jerks walking around with their electric . . . bongos! I mean, I can't go through a single day without running into one of them, and they all think they're so superior to me, that's what really gets me. They all think they're musical geniuses. You should see them." He looked at the therapist from the corners of his eyes. "Do you know what I'm saying?"

"Yes, I understand," the therapist replied. He sat back in his rocking chair, an older man with thick-lensed glasses and a beard. "I was just wondering about your brother. I was wondering whether you ever expressed your anger at him—or at your mother for playing him against you."

"I don't know. Yeah, I remember once yelling at my mother and she said to me, 'Don't ever raise your voice to me like that. We could always give you away, you know.'"

"What did you say then?"

"I don't remember. Nothing, probably. My mother had this thing about being a good mother. She never wanted to hear anything that suggested she wasn't a good mother. If you said anything at all like that she'd treat you as though you were a traitor. As though you were really bad. She was always telling me I was overreacting or that I was oversensitive. Do you think I'm oversensitive?" The therapist started to answer but as usual was cut off. "Sure, I'm oversensitive. It's the price I have to pay for being an artist. To be an artist is to suffer. Artists have to suffer because of their sensitivity. But I'm not talking about these no-talent jerks. They don't suffer. I'm talking about *real* artists. Look at all the artists, writers, musicians throughout history who went mad, who lived tragic lives. They always suffered; at least the great ones did. It goes hand-in-hand with artistic sensitivity."

Artistic sensitivity. Again and again he would come back to that. Month after month he would explain about the music scene and suffering and artistic sensitivity. Now and then the therapist would venture a question, an interpretation, a gesture, but the patient did not seem interested in what the therapist thought; he was more interested in explaining about art and suffering so that the therapist could understand it. He wanted the therapist to be a narcissistic extension of himself, a part of his grandiose self, which would look noddingly on at whatever the patient said or did. So the therapist listened, nodded, and waited.

Finally, after several years of this, in the middle of one of his long explanatory sessions, the patient ran out of words. He had been talking about artistic sensitivity again, but not with the same degree of certainty. Now he sat glancing at the therapist uneasily, an expression of confusion on his face. He was silent for a while.

"What's going on?" the therapist asked.

"I was just wondering . . . what *you* think."

"What I think about what?"

"I was wondering . . . if you think . . . artists are more sensitive than the average person?"

It was the first time the patient had ever allowed the therapist to be anything but a "yes man." He took the opening, keeping the discussion on an abstract level, since that seemed to be all the patient could handle at the moment. Slowly and deliberately he pointed out to him the distinction, as he saw it, between artistic sensitivity and neurotic sensitivity. He spoke at some length about how artistic sensitivity was a positive quality that served to make artists more attuned to things such as truth and beauty. It was something they were born with—eyes that could see color and form; ears that could hear sounds in harmony; hearts that could feel the pulse of the unconscious. He compared an artist to a finely tuned instrument such as a microscope that could see to the depth of things; he was deliberately attempting to feed the patient's grandiosity in order that he might listen to the next part of the explanation. The patient's eyes were alert as the therapist spoke of these things, and he nodded quickly and said, "Yes, yes, I know what you're saying." This kind of sensitivity, artistic sensitivity, did not involve suffering, the therapist added in a slow, deliberate way, looking pointedly at the patient. The patient began to look less alert.

Neurotic sensitivity, on the other hand, was the cause of a great deal of suffering and often prevented artists from utilizing their artistic sensitivity and fulfilling themselves, the therapist continued. Neurotic sensitivity was an overreaction to one's present life circumstances due to the unresolved feelings of the past. To illuminate this point, the therapist made up a story of a woman who had a little sister who was always considered by their father to be prettier than she was, so that all her life the women felt inferior to her sister and jealous of her and neurotically sensitive to remarks about her appearance. She was always suffering because of her feelings of inferiority. The therapist watched the patient closely as he related this story and the patient's eyes appeared quite thoughtful. The therapist assumed he was reaching him at last. "So you see," the therapist concluded, "you don't have to suffer to be an artist. If anything, suffering blocks you from realizing your full potential as an artist."

There was a meditative silence. Then the patient sat up in his chair with a wide-eyed expression, and he nodded slowly as though a dawning were taking place somewhere among the synapses of his brain.

"Yes, yes, I know exactly what you're saying," he replied animatedly. "That's exactly what I've been trying to explain to you. I'm not oversensitive like my mother thinks. I have artistic sensitivity. I'm not utilizing my artistic sensitivity though, and so I'm suffering. And meanwhile, all these no-talent jerks, they're the ones who're neurotic. Now I understand them better," he said. "All this time I thought maybe it was me. Oh, well, it's a good thing I have my music. I don't know what I'd do without my music. It's everything to me. Everything."

The therapist was crestfallen, thinking the intervention had failed. However, the first thing the patient asked during the next session was, "So you think I'm suffering because I'm neurotic, is that it?"

Intervention 45

The Patient Who Sodomized His Wife

Ordinarily this middle-aged man did not have much difficulty in talking about sexual matters. However, one day he became evasive in describing sexual intercourse with his wife. In the three years of his three-times-a-week analysis, he usually spoke of sexual matters matter-of-factly but in boastful detail. Today there was more emotion, but hardly any detail. He was obviously embarrassed.

"You seem embarrassed," the therapist noted.

"I guess it's hard for me to say this. But this morning, well, I screwed my wife in the ass. I don't know why." He paused again.

"Was it fun?" The therapist knew from the patient's tone that it had not been much fun, and that he was smitten by conflicts about it. By asking a question he knew would be provocative, he hoped to dislodge the patient's real feelings about the episode.

"Fun?" the patient answered. "I guess so. All I know is I found myself wanting to screw her hard in the ass. She didn't really want to do it and I kind of forced her. I enjoyed forcing her. I wanted to burst into her, tear her, hurt her. Maybe I was angry with her about something. Or maybe I was angry at somebody else."

"Somebody else?"

The patient had been in analysis long enough to be able to make associations quickly, with only the slightest help from the therapist. "My mother. She called me yesterday," he said. "Yeah, I'm angry at her and my sister." During the rest of the hour and in the next session he was able to understand that the woman he had had anal intercourse with was, symbolically, his mother, whose womb he wanted to tear into in order to destroy his baby sister, who had been born when he was 3. He had never before understood both his hatred of his mother and of his sister with such depth of insight and feeling.

Intervention 46

An Oedipal Dream
and Its Interpretation

"My mother and I entered a room where my father was standing. I embraced my mother. My father looked solemn, as if he were angry at my mother for arriving late. I wanted to protect her with my embrace." The patient who related this dream was an analytic candidate in his late thirties who had been in analysis for four years and had already substantially worked through the pregenital material. Now the Oedipus complex had emerged and for several months the patient had become more resistant to hearing the analyst's interpretations. Basically this was the result of his reluctance to accept a passive-feminine position in regard to the therapist.

Because of the patient's resistance to interpretations, the therapist analyzed the dream in silence. He knew that he himself was the father in the dream. As for the patient's embracing his mother, the therapist interpreted that it was actually the patient's feminine part he was embracing, holding away from the father-therapist, thus resisting the union with him. The patient, as a jealous son, did not allow the mother within him to unite with the father-therapist, did not allow himself to be submissive to the father-therapist. Furthermore, the patient's resistance had to do with defending against the primal scene between the mother within him and the father-therapist (that is, against his homosexual feelings). Finally, the dream may also have been prophetic, as the patient had been late for the session just as the mother had been late in the dream.

"What do you make of it?" the therapist asked. He wanted to let the patient get as far as he could before venturing his own interpretation.

"I think it's about how I used to feel as a kid. I had such a strong identification with my mother," he replied rather glibly. "It was always my mother and me against my father. And he'd be angry." He continued in this vein, avoiding implications with respect to the analytic situation.

The therapist joined the resistance and asked for an elaboration about the patient's relationship with his father.

"I loved him and I hated him," the patient said. "He always seemed angry at me. I hated him for being angry, but I wanted his love and approval." He was silent for a moment.

"What are you thinking?"

"I was remembering seeing my father walking around the house in his underwear. You could see his testicles hanging out. It was gross." He was silent again.

"What are you thinking now?"

"I was just remembering when I was 4 or 5 years old, and I used to jump on my parents' bed in the mornings as soon as I woke up, and I'd grab my father's penis and squeeze it and he would wake up."

"Why didn't you want to tell me those memories?"

"I was embarrassed."

"Why?"

"I was afraid of what you'd think."

"What did you think I'd think?"

"I don't know." The patient was blushing, lying on the edge

of the couch. "Maybe I thought you'd try to relate all this to you and me, as usual. I know I'm supposed to have homosexual feelings toward you. But I don't. I really don't."

"How would I try to relate the dream to homosexual feelings about me?"

"Oh, you'd probably say the father represents you and that because my mother and I are embracing I have a negative Oedipus complex. And you'd say the feelings of ambivalence, of love and hate, I feel toward my father I also feel toward you."

"And would that be true?"

The patient suddenly chuckled. "Probably."

By having the patient do most of the work himself while letting it appear that he, the therapist, had joined the resistance, the therapist allowed the patient to break through his passive-feminine defense. For the first time the patient began to speak frankly of his homosexual feelings and fantasies while also acknowledging his admiration and jealousy of the therapist.

Intervention 47

The Masochistic Mother

She was a middle-aged woman who was having problems with her adolescent son. She tended toward what René Spitz might have called "primary anxious overpermissiveness." This woman had a lot of unconscious hostility toward her son since he reminded her of her younger brother. Her brother was favored by both her parents, and they insisted that she join with them in their special treatment of him. So she fought against her aggression through a reaction formation of love and concern for the brother's health (an outgrowth of her unconscious desire to do away with him). When she had a son, she treated him the same way, compensating for her unconscious feelings of aggression through a primary anxious overpermissiveness. The result of such treatment was that the son, like her younger brother, was constantly acting out toward her in an attempt to get her to set limits for him and acknowledge him as a real person.

The mother came to her therapy session distraught over the latest episode of acting out by her son. She had been in therapy for several years but did not feel she had gotten a handle on what was going on between her son and her. "I feel so confused," she moaned. "He seems to hate me and I don't know why. I just don't know what to do about him. I feel like running away."

The therapist, a woman of about the same age, offered the following interpretation. "You're confused because you're conflicted. Part of you knows your son is abusing you, and that you should punish him in order to teach him to respect you. However, the other part of you thinks that would be cruel. Whenever your brother acted that way, your parents would laugh it off, and on the rare occasions when you complained about him your parents would say you were making too much of it. You didn't learn to assert your feelings then, and you're not sure you have a right to assert them now and you're not sure you're seeing things correctly. Your son recognizes your conflict about discipline and this encourages him to try more provocative behavior."

This interpretation, repeated in differing forms, gradually helped the patient to acknowledge her own aggression and learn how to deal with it in a healthy way. The therapist was able to verbalize for the patient the conflict that lay at the core of her confusion. It expressed both conflicting trends and an explanation for the patient's inability to act satisfactorily on her seemingly more reasonable motive—the wish to punish her son. It also included a brief historical reconstruction and explained the result of her conflict—further acting out by the son. By interpreting both sides of the conflict, the therapist demonstrated her own neutrality to the situation (rather than siding with either the mother or the son). Had she interpreted only one side of the conflict ("You're afraid to punish your son because you'll feel guilty") the patient might have felt that she was pressing her toward a particular action. Furthermore, the therapist showed she understood how the patient was feeling; this was an indirect expression of empathy. If an interpretation captures the way a patient feels, it will most likely have a greater impact. In essence, the therapist provided a blueprint that allowed the patient to resolve the conflict on her own.

Intervention 48

Stages of Recovery
for an Oral Patient

During the various points of her therapy, a young woman who suffered from depression and overeating found different ways of resisting the therapist and acting out her transferences. In the beginning she was often dejected and silent, withholding herself from him and protecting him and herself from her pent-up aggression. The therapist discovered that the best intervention at the time was to ask a question or make a comment that demonstrated his concern. If he talked, it meant he was willing to "feed" her and would not abandon her. She would then be able to produce. If he did not talk, she reported feeling empty and forlorn, a way she had undoubtedly felt as an infant. Later in the therapy she began to view the therapist as a sexual object, and the father-transference was acted out. Yet there was still an oral-narcissistic substructure in effect. She reported strong sexual impulses toward the therapist and spent her sessions bantering and flirting with him in an effort to provoke him into some kind of sexual play—even if it were only verbal. If the therapist attempted to analyze this behavior, she was put off. Indirectly she let him know that she would not cooperate unless he first demonstrated some reciprocity of sexual feelings. At this point the intervention that worked best was for the therapist to acknowledge that he found the patient attractive (she had lost weight by then), but that it was important for them to study the meaning of these feelings, both hers and his. Once again he had to "feed" her in order to advance the therapy, and he also had to allow her to feel a twinship with him (they would analyze not only her feelings toward him, but his toward her as well). Still later in the therapy she began lapsing into silences again. These silences differed from those that had marked her beginning phase, in that the beginning silences were those of a forlorn, hapless individual who did not know what to say, while the later silences were characterized by stubborn defiance. The therapist understood that now she was ready to begin verbalizing her aggression (that is, acting out her negative mother- and father-transference), but that she needed the therapist's permission to do so. He decided that the most effective intervention was to prod her in a provocative way: "That's right, just sit on all that shit inside you and see what happens."

"Fuck you."

"Is that a term of endearment?"

"Fuck you. Fuck you. Fuck you."

They got into many a battle, and out of these battles grew a deepening understanding and love between therapist and patient. Now there was an intense involvement by the patient in the process of her therapy, akin to the involvement of a lover. This involvement with her therapist helped to advance the work of transference and resistance analysis, and they were able to proceed at a much faster pace with both reconstruction and working through. Eventually the woman had worked through enough of her oral fixations so that she no longer needed the therapist to feed or prod her and was carrying on the analysis with little help from him. That, of course, had been his aim all along.

Intervention 49

The Unhappy Homosexual

During his four years in therapy a young man struggling with ego-dystonic homosexual impulses and depression used to have a recurring memory. He was about thirteen, fat, and emotionally backward, and had awakened to discover he had had a wet dream. He darted out of his room and into the bathroom, where his father was standing before the mirror shaving. He told his father what had happened and was about to show him when his father gave him a look of disdain and said, "What do you want me to do? It's not my fault you're a man." This memory epitomized what their relationship had been over the years. The father had continually scoffed at the son, complaining that his mother had turned him into a "sissy." The son felt rejected and abandoned, yet he could not allow himself to feel angry at the father. Whenever he remembered this incident, he felt ashamed. It was his fault that his father rejected him; he was a jerk.

His therapist, a woman of about middle age who was eclectic in her approach to therapy, tried in many different ways to get the patient in touch with his anger toward his father, but to no avail. He had so thoroughly introjected the father's attitude toward him that he could not find the ego strength to separate from that introjection and externalize the anger.

Finally the therapist found a way. He sat before her one day complaining, as he often did, about his homosexual impulses. "I hate being homosexual. I feel so screwed up sexually. I feel so inadequate, like such a jerk." He sighed, his head bowed in depression and self-abnegation. "I don't know, I don't know, I don't know . . . all I know is I hate being this way."

The therapist waited a moment for the silence to set in. Then she said in a half-whisper: "It's not my fault you're a man."

The patient looked up, startled, and then his face fell into his hands and he began to cry. He shook his head slowly and the crying grew fierce. "Why couldn't he try to understand me! Why! He didn't even try! That asshole! God, I hate him! God, oh God, I hate him!"

Intervention 50

A Problem with Penis Envy

"When am I supposed to fall in love with you?" she asked playfully, her hands folded behind her head as she lay langorously on the couch. She was a dark-haired, dark-eyed beauty straight out of a romantic novel, a woman who had fallen in and out of love countless times with countless tall and handsome strangers. Her pattern was to seduce and conquer with her phallic vagina and then to abandon her prey for the next challenge. Her identification was with the aggressors, her father and brother, and her pattern was their pattern. Naturally, during the beginning phase of therapy she tried to recreate the pattern with her male therapist.

The therapist, who was not really the stuff of romantic novels—a tall and gangly man in his mid-thirties with a plain but sensitive face—understood the pattern but chose not to interpret it. He did not feel she was ready to hear an interpretation, nor to explore the masculinity complex that lay beneath. Instead, he asked, "What gave you the idea you're supposed to fall in love with me?"

"I was talking to a friend of mine this weekend. She was in analysis and she said she fell in love with her analyst. She said that was what was supposed to happen if the analysis was working well."

"Actually," the therapist replied, "there's no set rule about developing any particular feelings toward an analyst. Your instructions are simply to allow your feelings to come up as they will, and then we'll study them. You may feel love, hate, jealousy, indifference, all kinds of things." He did not want to encourage her in any particular direction. Had he done so, he would have become an accomplice in her pattern and an easy conquest. She might then have pretended to fall in love with him—at his bequest—and later complained that he had seduced her, which would have given her an excuse to leave him.

For a year she assaulted him with flirtation. She was so unrelenting that more than once he found himself flirting back. She was disarming and at times even entrancing. However, for the most part he was able to handle the feelings of lust and rage she aroused, now and then venturing an object-oriented question such as, "What effect do you intend to have on me when you tell me I have cute eyes?" She always replied flippantly that she was just being friendly. Whether or not she was aware of her deeper motives of wanting to seduce and conquer him, she would never acknowledge that to him. She seemed to understand herself quite well, freely talking about her pattern with men, easily admitting to being a seductress. But she consistently and adamantly denied having any such designs on the therapist. The therapist had become, for her, the untrustworthy older brother who had time and time again pretended to be nice only to set her up for the next betrayal; and also the father who had promised but never delivered his love. She was an hysteric stuck in a paranoid position. The therapist could scarcely reach her.

After a year of flirting with the therapist and getting no response, she started an affair with a man she said had been "thoroughly analyzed." She used this analyst-surrogate to act out her transference toward the real therapist. After a few months she reduced her weekly sessions from three to two a week and spent a considerable portion of her remaining sessions making provocative comments designed to torment the therapist.

"Jim's so sensitive and insightful," she would say about her new lover, her hands folded behind her head as usual. "In a way, it's like I have two analysts now. This morning I told Jim a dream and he made a terribly good point about my father. He said my father always gave me double messages. And you know, he did. But I'd never thought about it in quite that way before. Actually, I was thinking on my way here that I don't really need you anymore. I've got another analyst now." She turned her head around to glance at the therapist, grinning. "Now don't get serious on me. I'm only joking. I'm not really going to leave therapy."

"You seem angry at me," he said.

"What makes you think that?"

"You seem to want to get rid of me."

"I knew you were going to get serious. I was just joking."

"You know in analysis there's no such thing as 'just joking'."

"Yes, you keep saying that, but I'm not sure I believe it. I really don't want to get rid of you. I admire and respect you. You've helped me a lot. It's just that I don't need you as much anymore." She sighed rapturously, stretching out her arms so that the brass bracelets on her wrist jangled. "What can I tell you? I'm in love."

She kept up the affair with the analyst-surrogate for more than a year—much longer than her usual involvements—while continuing her rejecting behavior toward the therapist. His attempts to analyze her behavior were doomed to failure. Eventually he stopped trying to interpret, realizing that in this instance his need to analyze was an enactment of his countertransference; she had become his rejecting mother, whom he wanted to get back at by "slapping her hands" through the use of psychoanalytic jargon. At any rate, there was something inexorable about her behavior, a spiteful, manic rage that could not be stopped. When he understood these things he backed off and remained silent much of the time, letting her ramble on. Sometimes he joined her in her adulation of her boyfriend or agreed with her that perhaps she did not need him anymore. This new intervention succeeded in deflating her and advancing the therapeutic work.

She tired of the analyst-surrogate and disposed of him as she did all the men she became involved with—unflinchingly. She went through a series of other men, but none really interested her. She became more and more depressed. She was now well into the middle phase.

"I had a dream last night," she said one day in a sad, empty tone of voice. "I dreamed I was under water, in a cage. There was a man beside me. Suddenly a shark came out of nowhere and bit the man's leg. He was screaming but nobody could hear. I didn't really care." She paused, lying lazily on the couch. It was a quiet summer afternoon and the rays of the sun shot through the blinds and formed lines across her body, horizontally, like prison bars. "My period's late again," she continued in the same lifeless voice. "I hope I'm not pregnant. You know, I think the shark was a red shark, red-brown, like menstrual blood. It wasn't really a shark, though, more like one of those monsters in the paintings of Hieronymus Bosch. I think I'm like that. If I were a painting, I'd be full of all kinds of monsters and demons." She paused again. "Sometimes I think there's something wrong down there, something repulsive inside me. Reminds me of the feelings the man had in *La Boheme*, the man who felt repelled by his lover's consumption." She paused again. "Why don't you say something?"

"You feel something's wrong down there," the therapist said. "That there's a monster down there. I wonder if what you're really talking about is your resentment and anger about men's penises and your disgust with your vagina."

"Penis envy, penis envy, penis envy," the patient replied. "You're so typically Freudian."

"You wouldn't want to have a penis?"

"God, no! The thought of having a penis sickens me! Why

would I want one of those horrible, smelly things?" She paused and thought about it for a moment. "But I must admit I sometimes have a fantasy, a desire to out-fuck every man I meet. And sometimes I think if I had a penis I'd really show them how to use it. Most of them don't even know how to use them."

Another year passed. The patient's defenses were no longer as effective, and her resentment toward the therapist mounted. She could no longer act out her feelings the way she once had, no longer flirt with him, torment him, or withdraw into depression or silence. She had regressed to a pregenital dependency. There was no way out, and her archaic feelings were emerging with all their intensity. It was around the middle of her fourth year of therapy. She came in saying she felt agitated about something the therapist had said during the previous session.

"You and your textbook analysis," she scolded him as she threw herself onto the couch. Even her movements at this point had become childlike. "Penis envy, that's all you sexist male therapists ever think about," she said in a pouty voice. "You know, I was afraid to come here today. I was afraid I'd start screaming or lose control and . . . do something to you."

"What would you like to do to me?" he asked, matter-of-factly.

She fell into a sullen silence. He let her be. Fifteen minutes passed. She began to turn this way and that, now and then wiping beads of sweat from her forehead. Her face was pale, and her black hair dangled over the side of the couch in disarray. As the silence mounted, so did her agitation. She wanted the therapist to say something so that she could frustrate him with her silence the way he frustrated her with his. He knew this and waited. Finally she exploded.

"You want to know what I'd like to do to you? I'll tell you what I'd like to do. I'd like to bite your penis off. That's what I'd like to do. I'd like to bite it off and grind in into the floor, into your new rug. How do you like that? Is that Freudian enough for you? Are you satisfied? I hate you! I hate you! I HATE YOU!" She covered her face with her hands and stayed motionless for a minute. Then she uttered in a small, spiteful, childish voice, "I want your penis, I want it, I want it! And I'm going to get it. It's mine! Mine!" She began to sob with all her might, like a child.

The therapist waited until she had stopped before explaining to her what had happened. "You've just gotten in touch with some very old feelings, feelings you once had toward your father and brother and had to keep hidden all these years." For the first time, she really heard him.

Intervention 51

The Man with Womb Envy and the Pregnant Therapist

"I find myself doing something lately that I've never done before," a male patient told his female therapist. "I find myself filling my lungs to capacity, you know, while I'm sitting watching television or something. And then I hold the air in as long as I can. And then—this is the weird part—I feel as though something, some part of my body, should be eliminated. I can't really describe it, but I feel a pleasurable sensation when I do it."

The man had been in therapy for three years and had, for the most part, defended against intimacy with his therapist by filling each of his sessions with emotionless chatter. The therapist, an object relationist, listened with a great deal of empathy and tried to provide a facilitating environment. Her attempts at analyzing the patient's relationship with her were met with polite acceptance but were not really heard. He was an extremely passive man, who had felt abandoned by his mother soon after his birth, as she then had a succession of other children.

His therapist, who was in her sixth month of pregnancy, sat silently across the room, facing the patient. It was unusual for him to bring something to her attention as he had just done, and she wondered about the meaning of this new behavior. At that

141

moment she felt the growing organism moving inside her own body, and she understood. By filling his lungs to capacity and then imagining he was eliminating something, the patient was trying to experience himself giving birth. His resistance to her had been to a large extent the result of womb envy and the associated fear of castration. Unconsciously he envied and resented the power of his mother's vagina to give birth and to rule over the household; and through the talion principle, he feared castration by the envied and resented object. On an even more archaic level, he also feared re-engulfment by the omnipotent mother of infancy.

"How about doing it now?" the therapist asked the patient, taking an active approach. She felt that if she could get the patient to do the exercise while sitting facing her, he might become aware of its meaning on his own.

"You mean take a deep breath . . . now?"

"Sure."

"I'd be embarrassed to do it in front of you."

"How come?"

"I don't know. Why do you want me to do it?"

"It might help us to understand something."

"Well, if you think it'll help . . . ."

"I do." She smiled and nodded encouragingly.

He sat up in his chair and began to take in his breath. As soon as he had done so he exhaled in a puff and sank back into his chair, giggling like a young boy. He glanced at the therapist's belly, then at her eyes, then at the floor.

"What?" she asked.

"Now I know why I'm embarrassed."

"Why?"

"Because *I* want to have a baby! Isn't that ridiculous? I'm jealous of you because you're pregnant." He giggled some more and a few tears sprang into his eyes.

"Do you think this is a new feeling brought on by my pregnancy, or has it been there before?"

"No, it's always been there, I think. Yes, it's always been there. I can remember feeling that way as a child. I can remember having those feelings about my mother. Each time she was pregnant I'd feel envious, abandoned, and angry. . . ."

His defensive chatter had, for the moment, vanished.

Intervention 52

The Therapist Who Joined
a Psychotic's Delusion

Night after night a man who was in a mental institution (where he had been for several years) had persecutory delusions. He would wake up in a panic, climb on the furniture of his room, and plead with his persecutors to please let him live. He would plead in different languages for they were all powerful spies from foreign lands. Invariably by daybreak he would succeed in saving his life and would sink, exhausted, into his bed. Only the nurses knew of these nightly delusionary experiences, for he himself did not remember them upon waking. His therapist, a woman psychiatrist, knew of the delusions by way of the nurses; however, each time she attempted to broach the subject with the patient, he did not understand what she was talking about.

The therapist had not been able to make much headway with the patient in the four years she had worked with him, and she decided that in order to do so she had to somehow penetrate his delusions. She had the nurses awaken her the next time his delusional experience began. When she got to his room, he was dashing here and there, climbing on top of his chest of drawers, on various chairs, on the windowsill, and on the bed. His movements were nervous, awkward, and his hair stuck out in different directions as though he had just been electrocuted. He was pleading with imaginary people in Engligh, German, Hungarian, and French.

"Was ist los?" she asked the patient. *"Ich helfe dich!"* She began speaking to the persecutors in German—the only other language she knew besides English—telling them to get away before she called the guards. The patient looked from her to the space where the imaginary attackers were perched, shaking his head incredulously. After about fifteen minutes he quieted down. He slept peacefully for the rest of the night.

The therapist had to repeat this performance a few more times before she succeeded in breaking through the wall separating the delusion and the real traumatic experiences that had engendered it. Once that had happened, the path was open to the analysis of his transference psychosis and of his extreme form of resistance.

Intervention 53

The Patient Who Assaulted His Therapist

For many years a male patient struggled with his fear of expressing his rage at his female therapist. He could express it indirectly, by writing bad checks or falling asleep during sessions, but he could never do it directly. He had never been able to express rage directly to any woman, beginning, of course, with his mother.

"The only way I've ever been able to express direct anger to a woman," he told her toward the end of a session, "is if I'm drunk."

"What happens when you're drunk?" she asked.

"I guess I lose my inhibitions. I no longer feel I have to protect women. I let it all hang out."

"What would you say to me if you were drunk?"

He was silent for a moment. "I guess I'd start by telling you I really hate your guts." He stopped, as though surprised at himself. He continued with more intensity. "Actually, I really do hate your guts. I don't know why. But I do, and since you asked me, I don't mind telling you I do. In fact, it feels kind of good to tell you." He glanced at her from the couch. "In fact, fuck you!

You want to know what I'd say? I'd say fuck you!" He banged the wall with his fist and yelled out, "Cunt! Cunt! Cunt! Uppity fucking cunt!" He began banging the wall and kicking the couch with his heels. "I hate your fucking guts, you cunt! And I hate your dirty hole! How do you like that?" The therapist was silent. Her silence seemed to enrage him further. "I asked you a question. How do you like it, cunt?" The therapist was tempted to say something, but she held back, knowing that when a patient was into such feelings it was best to remain silent until the fit had run its course. "Well, that's too bad if you don't like it!" he snapped, jumping up from the couch. He lunged at the therapist, as though to strike her; she sat calmly observing him, looking neither frightened nor menacing. He grabbed her shoulders and shook her, smiling fiendishly. "You really think you're clever, don't you? Well, you're not so clever! You're not so clever at all!" He whirled around and was about to storm out of the door.

She called out his name, calmly, empathically.

He turned, looking at her with disbelief.

"Would you do me a favor?" she said with respect in her voice and manner. "Would you mind staying and finishing out the session so we could talk about what just happened?"

Slowly he began to relax. Then he shook his head, thoughtfully, and lay back down on the couch. He began to cry.

"Why were you crying?" she asked afterward.

"When you didn't get angry at me for telling you off . . . when you heard everything I said and still cared about me, it made me sad. I could never yell at my mother that way. I could never tell her anything I really felt; if I did, she'd never speak to me again. I wasn't telling you off, I was telling off my mother. And you know what? I no longer feel like a little boy pretending to be a man." Tears slid down his cheeks.

The therapist's use of psychodrama (asking him what he would say to her if he were drunk), silence, and empathy were instrumental in the patient's overcoming his block with respect to expressing anger directly to a woman. Similar interventions would have to be repeated before the patient would grow comfortable doing so, but this was a start.

It is particularly difficult for female therapists to withstand the rage of their male patients, yet all important that they do so. Unless patients, male or female, can feel free to express their rage to their therapists, they cannot progress to the deepest levels of therapy. Of course, each therapist must judge for himself or herself whether a patient is capable of violence and must design these interventions accordingly. The more potential for violence a therapist perceives in a patient, the more necessary it is to reiterate the rules against no violence and, in fact, against moving from the couch or chair during a session.

Intervention 54

The Patient Who Saw Monsters
from the Couch

A schizophrenic patient steadfastly refused to lie on the couch, and her therapist did not insist on it. However, every so often he would bring up the subject in order to explore her resistance about doing so. She would always reply that she was afraid of losing control going crazy—if she lay on the couch. The therapist understood that what she was really afraid of was that her rage would explode and overwhelm her and the therapist. For four years the stalemate over the couch continued. Finally, she agreed to try it.

"How does it feel?" he asked.

She lay stiffly, her legs spread out and her arms at her sides, as though about to submit to some form of torture. "It feels . . . funny." Without moving her head, she gazed about the room, her eyes darting here and there. "Everything seems darker . . . menacing . . . ." The therapist asked if she was all right, and she said she was. She finished the session without complaint. "That was interesting. I think I'd like to try it again," she said as she departed.

An hour before her next appointment she left a message on the therapist's answering machine. "I've decided to quit therapy," she said in a nervous voice. "Thanks for all you've done for me."

The first thing he asked her when he called her back was, "What were you feeling when you were lying on the couch?" He knew that something had happened while she was on the couch, and the only way to get her back into therapy was to have her talk about it. At first she denied her feelings and assured him her decision was based on money matters. But when he pressed her, she admitted, "I can't come back to your office again. It's haunted. When I was lying on the couch, I saw things ... faces ... monsters." He let her go on for fifty minutes, then asked her to come back for the following session. "You can sit in a chair again, and we can even leave the door of the office open if you like." She liked that.

When she returned, the therapist used the experience to help the patient understand that the monsters were grotesque images of her mother, whom she felt was disapproving of her lying on a couch in a man's office – an act of blatant carnality in her mother's eyes. The patient was then able to get a sense of the depth of her rage at her mother and of how she projected it onto the environment. In general, therapists must do whatever is necessary – as in this case, extending a free telephone session – in order to keep a patient in therapy and advance the process.

Intervention 55

The Reluctant Debutante
and the Therapist Who Listened

She did not really think she had problems to speak of, and she said she was kind of embarrassed to be in therapy. After all, she had always had everything she wanted, so what was there to complain about? Her parents were wealthy, she had grown up in an exclusive suburb of Philadelphia, and been doted on by nannies and maids, had attended private schools and colleges, had come out at the debutante's ball, had traveled widely through Europe and the Far East, had oodles of friends in high places, was pretty and bright, and could have her pick of numerous rich and handsome suitors. Yes, there was a bit of depression at times, but didn't everybody have that? And, yes, she tended to overeat in the middle of the night, and then to force herself to vomit, but she could live with that. And yes, she admitted she was kind of choosy about men, and now at the age of thirty-two she still had not found one who was right for her, even though a bevy of them had courted her. But lots of people were having the same trouble, weren't they?

She really did not have any right to complain, and she did not want to stay in therapy for long. There was just this one little thing she had never talked about with anybody before, and she

thought she would just do it now, before she went off to Europe
again in the spring. It wasn't all that important. It was something
that had happened when she was very young. Things that happened that far back didn't really affect you as an adult, she
thought. But still, it was time to talk about it with somebody. It
was about her uncle. When she was 3 and 4 and 5 and maybe 6
years old she used to stay at his ranch in the summers, and
sometimes he would come into her room late at night and pull up
her nightgown and do things to her. She could not remember
what it was, and she was sure it was not all that important. In
fact, she was not sure it had happened at all, or whether she had
imagined it. For when she had told her mother about it, her
mother had been convinced she had imagined it. And her mother
was always right about things like that.

Her therapist, an older woman, listened to the young woman's story and asked her to talk about it some more. She wanted
to know everything the patient remembered about the ranch,
about her uncle, about her brothers, about her parents, and about
her life at that time.

The debutante reluctantly agreed to continue talking about
it. She talked about it and talked about it. A year passed. She
remembered how tyrannical her mother was, and how she could
never talk with her, and also realized why it was so hard for her
to talk with the therapist. Another year passed. She remembered how distant and cold her father was, and how angry and
contemptuous she was because of the way he let her mother
dominate him. Another year passed. She wanted to kill her uncle,
her parents, and her therapist, but she realized that her therapist
was not her uncle or her parents. She cried a lot, and wondered
how she had ended up in therapy for three years. It was so
self-indulgent, and yet this memory had not wanted to go away.
Anyway, she had to admit she felt better. She had a steady
boyfriend, was less depressed, and did not overeat and vomit in
the middle of the night anymore. Actually, she was very grateful
to the therapist. She did not think she had ever before been

listened to the way the therapist had listened to her. Nobody—not her parents, not her brothers, not her friends, not her teachers—nobody had ever really listened, and she thanked her therapist for that, thanked her with her child-like heart and her adult heart. The therapist said she was welcome, and the patient said maybe therapy was not so self-indulgent after all; and she talked on.

Intervention 56

The Man Who Was Raped
by His Mother

Like many men, he had been sexually abused by his mother but did not know it. When a father sexually abuses a daughter, it is usually very obvious, for it is not generally his role to be physically intimate with his children. But a mother's sexual abuse can be very subtle: an extra amount of attention to bathing her son's genitals; insistence on enemas, particularly as a form of punishment; a flirtatious or castrating manner of relating to her son, which stifles his sexual growth. All these and other forms of behavior can be just as abusive and harmful to a son's development as a father's sexual molestation can be to a daughter's.

A male patient had talked with his female therapist many times about the enemas his mother had given him throughout his childhood. Though he remembered them as having been humiliating and painful, it had never occurred to him that he was angry at his mother about the enemas, or that she had behaved in an improper manner.

One day as he was talking about the enemas again in a rather emotionless way, the therapist threw in an interpretation. She wanted to reframe the event so as to enable him to view it more emotionally. Also, she understood that he needed permission to verbalize critical thoughts about his mother, permission that only she—as his transferred mother—could give him. So, when there was a lull in his session, she interspersed, somewhat bluntly, "Your mother raped you."

He replied, *"Raped* me?" as though trying out a new word. "I never thought of it that way." He fell silent for a moment, then said, "You know, I always felt there was something strange about those enemas. I mean, if I even looked like I was constipated, she'd give me an enema. So I'd always be so scared of getting an enema that I'd be constipated. I'd literally be scared shitless. I think she was angry at my father or at men, and she'd take it out on me. Yes, that makes sense. I did feel violated. She had no concern for my feelings when she did it. She was very rough, and if I complained she'd call me a sissy and say she hoped I'd learn my lesson. You know, I'm really angry at her about that. . . ."

Intervention 57

Color and the Emotions

"I hate it!"

"Hate what?"

"Hate working with colors. I wish I didn't have to. I wish I had never been commissioned to do this painting." There was a self-pitying whine in her voice, a forlorn expression in her eyes, a martyred stoop to her shoulders. "I don't know why I can't just stick with black and white drawings. I *like* doing drawings. I'm great at it. But deep inside I know I'll never respect myself as an artist unless I can master the use of color." She shook her head. "I really hate it."

She was a young artist who had come to therapy because, as she put it, she did not feel anything. Whenever her male therapist asked her during her once-a-week therapy sessions how she was feeling about her boss, her boyfriend, or about him, she would invariably reply she felt nothing. She reported only a numbness from her neck down. She thought feelings with her head but could not feel them in her body. As a result, she was not really connected to her art or to her life.

The therapist knew that the plight of this patient was typical of many visual artists. Because she had gotten out of touch with her emotions, she had also lost touch with her creativity and her capacity to use colors. To the extent that artists repress their emotions their use of color becomes limited or distorted—colors being visual representations of emotions. For the first year of therapy the patient focused almost entirely on this one issue, since her salvation rested upon her success as an artist. Through fame she would demonstrate to her family the humanity and specialness they had ignored or stifled; or so she thought.

"What happens when you try to work in color?" the therapist asked her one day, hoping to enable her to understand what feelings were blocked.

"I just . . . clamp up," she said. She sat before him, her head nodding as usual. "I don't have any confidence. I keep going over and over the faces, can't seem to get the noses right, or the mouths . . . and I can't do the shadows at all. It's ridiculous. When I paint in color I feel like a baby, as though I've never painted before. It's totally frustrating and humiliating."

For years she struggled with this as well as with other interrelated issues. During that time the therapist was able to gain an understanding of how she had formed the habit in early childhood of numbing her emotions. As a child she had been weaned rather early by a mother who had not particularly wanted a girl child; then she had been terrorized by parents who were constantly violent with one another and with her. If she had ever tried to express any of her fear or anger, she had been told to "stuff it, or I'll give you something to really cry about!" On occasion her father, an electrician, had whipped her with electrical wire. The terror and rage of those days were associated in her unconscious with the color red, her loneliness with the color blue, and the tenderness that had been missing was associated with the color yellow. Her inability to use those and other colors was an avoidance of the feelings and memories they would stir.

As the working-through process began to make inroads into these repressed emotions and memories, she reported occasional flashes of anger, fantasies of revenge, and hints of sadness. This represented much progress for her, for until then she had experienced only numbness or anxiety—nothing else. However, she still could not effectively use color. The breakthrough came one day when the therapist decided to use an experiential exercise.

"Are you feeling numb today?" he asked.

"I suppose so. I don't feel anything, so I guess I must be numb."

"I'd like to try an experiment. I want you to make yourself even more numb."

"Why?"

"Maybe you're not numb enough to really block out all your feelings. Maybe you need to make yourself even more numb. Just trust me and see what happens. I want you to deliberately concentrate on numbing yourself."

She sat up in her chair, shaking her head. "All right, if you say so." She stiffened herself, staring at the therapist as she did so. "This feels funny," she said.

"Funny?"

"Pins and needles all over."

"Do it even more."

"I don't know if I can."

"You can. You've been doing it all your life. You're a master at it."

The patient gritted her teeth. She began to shake. "What's happening?" she asked.

"Keep going."

"I'm . . . scared." She began to sob, then to cry.

Afterwards, she spoke with more feeling about her abusive childhood. As she did so, her capacity for using color gradually began to grow. Joining her resistance and giving her permission to numb herself had taken away her unconscious reason for doing so. This was her first release from the bondage of her narcissism. There would be many others.

Intervention 58

The Patient Who Wanted
To Lose Weight

Year after year she spoke of her weight problem. Year after year she seemed incapable of doing anything about it. Year after year, her therapist, a classical analyst, attempted to analyze the psychic conflicts beneath the symptom. The problem had first appeared during adolescence, with the onset of menstruation. It had to do with her fear of sex and intimacy with men, and on a deeper level with her anger at her father and fear of competition with her mother. The condition had been reinforced when her father continually called her "pig" and her mother warned her that she would never be as popular as she herself had been in school if she did not lose weight. The therapist had provided her with a basic understanding of the foundation of the problem and with an understanding of how the weight helped her to avoid relationships in her present life and also to avoid the unpleasant feelings of envy, sadness, and rage inside her. He had also helped her to make progress in other respects: She went from living on unemployment to being able to accept the responsibility of a steady job; she returned to night school to finish work on her B.A.; and she established an ongoing relationship with a man 20 years older—the first relationship she had ever had. Yet her weight problem persisted.

Finally, on the advice of his supervisor, the therapist decided to diverge from psychoanalytic procedure and use a behavioral intervention. The patient had complained one day that she was planning to go home for her high school reunion and would have to subject herself to comments about her weight. The therapist took the opportunity to introduce the new intervention.

"How much do you want to lose weight for the reunion?" he asked her.

"How much? I'd give anything to be able to do it."

"If you really want to do it, I have a surefire plan to enable you to accomplish it, and also save money for the reunion at the same time."

"How?" She looked around from the couch, her eyes alert.

He explained the plan to her. There were three months until the reunion. If she lost three pounds a week for 13 weeks, she would reduce her weight from its present 161 pounds to her normal weight of 120 pounds. She agreed that such a schedule of weight loss was in the realm of possibility. But she was skeptical. What would motivate her to do something she had never been able to do before? And what did he mean about saving money? He explained the rest of the plan: she would begin paying him an extra $25 per therapy session which, in 13 weeks, would accumulate to $325. If she got down to the prescribed weight of 120 pounds, she would get the money and could use it for her trip home. If she did not achieve the goal, the therapist would keep the money.

"Actually, I'm betting on the fact that you won't be able to do it," the therapist taunted her. "I need a little more money for my vacation this summer." He was deliberately mimicking her father.

The patient was duly challenged. Not only was she desirous of losing weight for all the obvious reasons; she was also motivated to lose it in order to defeat the therapist/father. The last thing she wanted was for him to keep her money, and his taunt about her not being able to do it was the final reinforcer. By the deadline she had gone down to 119 pounds. Along the way, she had been forced to confront her envy of and anger at the therapist, her father, and her mother, as well as her fear of intimacy with men and her aversion to their flirtation. Indeed, this behavioral intervention became a turning point of her therapy, bringing up much new material and greatly accelerating the analysis.

Intervention 59

The Battered Woman
Who Would Not Budge

When the female patient first came to see the therapist, who was a man about the same age, she told him she had just left a female therapist because that therapist had given her an ultimatum: either she leave her boyfriend, who frequently became violent, or she would have to find another therapist. "I decided to find another therapist," she said. "So here I am."

Within six months this therapist also felt like giving her an ultimatum. During that time the patient had filled her sessions with sorrowful complaints about her boyfriend. He had stabbed her in the leg; he had punched her in the eye; he had strangled her; he had kicked her; and he was mentally cruel to her. "I can't stand it," the patient said, lying haplessly on the couch, her husky voice choked with emotion. "I never have a moment's peace. Even when I'm at work, he calls me ten or twenty times a day, asking me what time I'll be home. And if I tell him I don't know, he keeps asking me again and again, like a worn-out record. Then if I give in and tell him I'll be home at such-and-such time, he'll call back and ask if I want him to have dinner ready. If I say I don't care, he'll say he has to have an answer. If I tell him yes, he'll ask me what I want for dinner. If I say I don't know, he'll ask me over and over until I tell him. He knows I don't want him to keep calling me, but he does it anyway, no matter what I say. It drives me crazy. Then when I come home I'm constantly crazed. I can't stand him. He constantly wants to touch me, constantly wants to have sex with me, even though I tell him I'm not interested. He keeps saying I really love him, but I'm too screwed up to know it. If I don't have sex with him, he'll start to cry and accuse me of being a cold bitch. Or he'll keep asking me over and over, 'Will you have sex with me after dinner?' I'll say, 'No.' He'll ask, 'Why?' I'll say, 'Because I don't want to.' He'll say, 'Why don't you want to?' I'll say, 'I keep telling you, I'm not turned on by you.' He'll say, 'If you're not turned on, why did you enjoy it so much the other night?' I'll say, 'I never enjoy it; that's your imagination.' He'll say, 'If I cook dinner and wash the dishes, will you have sex with me?' I'll say, 'No. I don't want to have sex with you, period.' He'll say, 'You really want to, but you just don't want to say it. You want me to just take you, like I always do.' He'll keep it up all night until I finally get so tired of his pressure that I give in. 'All right, go ahead and do it, but I'm not going to enjoy it. Then he'll do it and I'll hate it, I'll just hate it the whole time. I'll feel absolutely revolted by him." She began to sob, reaching for a tissue. "And then, like the other night, we have a violent fight and one of our neighbors calls the police. It's so embarrassing. I mean, he keeps pushing me, pushing me, pushing me, until I give in. And then he gets furious at me for not enjoying sex with him. And I feel like scratching his eyes out for forcing me. And that's what I did the other night; I tried to scratch his eyes out. And then he got angry and punched me in the stomach and knocked the breath out of me. I don't even care anymore if I live or die. I really can't stand it. I'm falling apart anyway. I keep grinding my teeth at night, and the dentist said if I don't stop he'll have to make me a bridge. I keep hyperventilating all day long. I'm smoking four packs a day. I keep feeling these pains in my heart, and I'm afraid I'm going to have a heart attack. I don't know what to do. I really don't know what to do."

The therapist, after listening to such a diatribe, would be full of anger at the patient's boyfriend. He would have fantasies of going to the apartment and telling him off and whisking the patient away. He had not been practicing very long, and he still found it difficult to control his countertransference. Also, he had come from a background of family violence. His father had been an alcoholic and abusive to his mother, who had worn her bruises like a mantle of righteousness. The therapist had continually been thrown in the middle of his feuding parents. Often he would have fantasies of whisking his mother away, fantasies similar to the ones he was now having about this patient.

"Why don't you leave him?" he would ask her again and again.

"I've tried leaving him and it doesn't work."

"Why?"

"Because no matter where I go, he'll find me. Then he'll call me twenty times a day and beg me to come back, and promise me if I come back he'll do this and he'll do that. Also, sometimes he says if I leave him he'll kill me and then he'll kill himself."

"You can get an order of protection."

"That won't do any good with him. He doesn't care about that. Anyway, I don't have anywhere to go. And I don't have the money to pay the rent and security on an apartment."

"You could move to a women's shelter."

"I wouldn't be caught dead in one of those places."

No matter what the therapist proposed, she always found a reason to invalidate it. He understood why she had become stuck in this relationship. She had known primarily abuse from an early age. Her stepfather had raped her in a closet when she was 4 (she now had an elevator phobia); her mother had put her into an orphanage when she was 6. In her teens she had gone through a succession of foster homes, again suffering mental and sexual abuse. Her therapist understood that her attraction to this man was an unconscious repetition of her relationship with her stepfather. In continually turning down her boyfriend's sexual advances, she was attempting to assuage her guilt feelings about successfully seducing her stepfather. Most little girls during the oedipal stage want to take their father away from their mother; however, when it actually occurs, it leaves a residue of guilt, as well as feelings of anger, betrayal, and low self-esteem. Such was the case with this patient. The therapist also understood that her inability to rise above a bare subsistance level was associated with her dependence all during her childhood on social institutions, whereas her reluctance to move into a women's shelter was due to the aversion she had developed to such institutions. He understood all this; nevertheless his frustration and anger mounted. He kept feeling there was something he ought to be doing and was not doing. These, of course, were the feelings of impotence she was arousing in him, feelings she too refused to fully acknowledge in herself or to do anything about.

With his supervisor's guidance, the therapist managed to control his countertransference and simply be there for the patient. The supervisor helped him to understand that what the patient wanted from him was for him to be a transitional object — an object with ears to listen and a heart to care, but with no mind to judge and no mouth to speak. So for the next year he just listened. Her ramblings did not allow him to get much of a word in anyway; indeed, there were many sessions in which he did not speak at all, and she did not notice. She seemed to be making headway, however, in some respects. Although she continued to work for temporary-help agencies, her jobs became more steady, and she began to learn new skills such as word processing. And she seemed, more and more, to be talking herself into leaving her boyfriend. Finally, after another night of violence, she did leave him. The empathic listening had worked.

She lived with a friend for several months. During that time, her elevator phobia became so acute that she could no longer accept temporary assignments in elevator buildings. This drastically limited the jobs that could be assigned to her, and her resources began to diminish. In the meantime, her boyfriend was calling her again and again, showing up at her doorstep, begging her, bribing her, charming her, bombarding her with flowers and other gifts, and in other ways inundating her with attention. She began discussing with the therapist whether or not she should return to him.

"Why would you want to move back in with him?" the therapist asked her as calmly as he could.

"I don't know. Sometimes I think I feel sorry for him."

"Why would you feel sorry for somebody who once stabbed you in the leg with a pair of scissors?"

"It's crazy, I know. But sometimes I see him as such a needy little boy. And, anyway, I don't know what else to do. I can't keep living off Judy. I don't know. He asked me to just try moving in with him for two weeks. He wants me to give it a two-week trial. What do you think?"

"Suppose I told you not to do it? Would you listen?"

"Yes, definitely."

The trouble was, the patient could not listen to the therapist. She was inexorably involved with her boyfriend, bonded to him as an infant is bonded to a rejecting mother. The therapist was seen as a lustful intruder. The more the therapist tried to reach out for her, the more she saw him in a critical way. Once he had offered to come with the police and remove her from the apartment himself. She had responded by questioning his ethics and bringing in a dream in which he was portrayed as a rapist. The therapist had learned to remain neutral. She went back to her boyfriend, immediately sank into a severe depression, and blamed the therapist for her misery.

"I feel like I'm getting worse," she told the therapist over and over. "I'm more depressed than I've ever been in my life. I can't sleep at night. I'm a wreck all day long. My dentist says the bones in my jaw are deteriorating. My doctor says if I don't stop smoking so much I'll die of lung cancer. I don't feel like getting out of bed in the morning. I don't feel like working. I don't feel like doing anything. And I wonder whether therapy is doing any good. Maybe I ought to be seeing a woman therapist. I mean, I've been seeing you for four years now and nothing's happening. Why can't I leave my boyfriend? I don't understand why I can't leave him. Do you understand? If you do, why won't you tell me?"

"We've gone over it many times, and each time I thought you understood. Now you say you don't understand."

"Tell me again."

"That's the problem. You want me to *tell* you. *You* have to discover it for yourself."

"Then why am I paying you?"

"To help you discover."

"I don't know. I don't know. I just don't seem to be moving. I'm in the same boat I was in when I first came to see you. I don't think I've accomplished anything at all. It seems as though you should have helped me to leave him by now."

"You *did* leave him. And then you moved back again, against my advice."

"But you could have done something to stop me."

"What?"

"I don't know. But there must be something. You're the shrink. How should I know?"

Around and around they went. Despite all his efforts, the patient was getting worse. Her depression was greater, her dependence on her boyfriend more complete, and her employment less steady. She hardly saw any of her girlfriends anymore, and she lived the life of a recluse, shuttling between work and home without any social activities. She was apparently more stuck than ever. The therapist again brought the case to the attention of his supervisor. The supervisor agreed that the case had all the earmarks of a negative therapeutic reaction. The patient was more than ever shifting the responsibility for her condition onto the therapist, and she was determined, unconsciously, to make him feel like a failure. Symbolically, she was castrating her stepfather and frustrating his sexual advances (she viewed the therapist's desire to help her leave her boyfriend as evidence that he himself had designs on her). She would even commit a slow suicide, as she was in fact now doing, if it would cause the therapist/father to suffer. Recognizing all this, the supervisor suggested that the therapist propose to the patient that perhaps he really was not the right therapist for her, and that maybe it was time to talk about his referring her to somebody else. By joining her resistance, the therapist would help her to discover that, yes, she really did want another therapist or, no, she did not really want another therapist and that something else was going on.

After the therapist made the proposal to the patient, she cut him off and took the opposing view. "I don't think I need another therapist," she said with a sudden burst of energy. "Are you trying to get rid of me?"

"No, not at all. But you've been saying maybe you need a woman therapist, and that you don't think you're making progress."

"Maybe I'm just going through a phase," she cut in again. "Don't patients go through phases now and then? Maybe it's a phase. Could that be it?" There was an urgency in her voice, and the depressive, listless demeanor that had enshrouded her for several months had vanished. "In fact, I was thinking maybe I ought to see you twice a week. I'll have to get more work, though, so I can afford it."

In the weeks that followed she flipped into a manic state, which allowed her to make the moves that were necessary. She took a permanent job for the first time in her life and started seeing the therapist twice a week. Six months later she had saved enough money to pay the security and rent for a furnished room. With the therapist's help, which she now accepted, she was able to break away from her boyfriend – gradually and painfully. The negative father transference had shifted into an idealizing mother transference, which enabled her to establish a kind of therapeutic alliance with him that made it possible for her to advance to the next step in her life and in her therapy. Now at last they would begin to sort out and resolve the conflicts that had led her into the abusive relationship in the first place.

Intervention 60

The Man Who Had Penis Envy

He was a middle-aged man who had spent more than 20 years in various forms of therapy with various kinds of therapists, and he had made some progress in each instance. Yet he felt there was something that had not been reached, and so he persisted.

One day as he was talking, as he usually did, about his sexual problems with his wife (he suffered from premature ejaculation), he brought up the term, "penis envy." At first he was speculating about his wife's penis envy, then his mother's. Then he remembered seeing his father's penis as a child and thinking how large it was in comparison with his own. The patient had covered this ground and made similar statements before, but this time it struck his therapist, an elderly but alert psychoanalyst, in a different way.

The therapist suddenly felt as though he were listening to a young female of about adolescent age instead of a man. And he understood that this female part of the man had been dissociated from the consciousness of his ego; that is, his female part was ego-dystonic. His concern about his wife's and mother's penis envy was a projection of his own penis envy—the penis envy felt by the girl inside of him, which he had disowned. All of this became even more understandable when the therapist recalled the man's memories of his childhood. He had been the second son of a mother who had wanted a girlchild. Therefore, when he was born, his mother saw him as a girl, and as he grew up she continued to treat him as one. In particular, she seemed never to have taken notice of the fact that he had a penis, and so on an unconscious level he felt as though his penis were invisible, or at least inadequate. He envied the way his father proudly carried his penis and held it in his hands when he urinated; his father enjoyed his penis in a way the son could not.

Having thought about all this, the therapist offered the following interpretation. "I feel as if I'm listening to a girl today. I feel as if I'm listening to a girl talking about penis envy."

"You know," the man replied right away, "I often feel like a girl. Like a young girl. But I never thought about it in quite that way. I mean, nobody's ever said to me they saw me as a girl. But you're right, I feel as though there's a little girl inside me." He thought for a moment, then chuckled. "If I were to tell anybody about this girl, they'd think I was crazy."

"Actually, it is I who see and hear a girl, when in fact there is a man on my couch. The crazy person is me."

"I'm glad you said that. That's right, *you* see me as a girl. My mother saw me as a girl. She's the crazy one, not me!"

The patient had finally reached the conflict that had haunted him for so many years, and about which he had spoken from various angles over that time. The therapist had deliberately framed his interpretation in a way that replicated the point of view of the patient's mother. By telling the patient that he viewed him as a girl, and that it was he who was crazy for viewing him that way, he was able to help the patient to understand and release himself from his introjected gender conflict.

Intervention 61

The Therapy "Nut" and the Psychodramatist

She had tried just about every form of therapy available—from psychoanalysis to primal therapy, from behavior modification to deep massage, and from bioenergetics to dance therapy. Finally she went to see a psychodramatist. "I've been through it all," she told the therapist, a woman who had once been an actress before she had trained in psychodrama, "and nothing works."

The psychodramatist was not the least discouraged. Without further ado, she placed a chair in the center of the room and asked the patient to imagine that she herself was seated in the chair. Then she instructed the patient to portray her therapists, one by one, beginning with the first. "Be your therapists," she told her. "What would each of them say to you now?" At first the woman did burlesques of each therapist, exaggerating their faults as she saw them. The psychodramatist asked her to do the exercise again, this time portraying each therapist in a more realistic way. Now the woman had a great deal of difficulty grasping what the psychodramatist wanted her to do. It was difficult for her to understand how to play her former therapists realistically, for in order to do so she would have to give up her paranoid projections. After a 20 minute discussion on how to do

172

it, the patient began to perform. Haltingly, she had the first therapist say, "I tried to help you . . . but . . . you're difficult to help." She stopped and looked at the psychodramatist, bearing a trace of sadness in her eyes.

"Tell her why she's difficult to help," the psychodramatist said.

"You're difficult to help . . . because . . . because . . . you won't let anybody in. You won't let anybody in . . . just like your mother didn't let *you* in." She broke into sobs and continued to interpret her own behavior. Now she could hear the interpretations that she had previously resisted hearing, for they were coming from herself. The patient ended up staying with the psychodramatist for a year, with productive results.

Intervention 62

The Schizophrenic Patient
Who Exploded

There comes a time during the therapy process with a schizophrenic patient when he will change from a rage-withdrawal to a
rage-combat posture. Often it takes many years of painstaking
work before the patient will establish both a therapeutic alliance
and an observing ego that are strong enough to enable such a
step. In addition, such a step requires a therapist who can
tolerate a schizophrenic's rage.

A man had been in therapy with a male therapist for seven
years before getting to this stage. During the seven years
leading up to the explosion, he had defended against his rage
through an attitude of apathy and indifference to other people,
particularly to the therapist. During those years the therapist
attempted to provide a safe, supportive environment that served
to strengthen the patient's ego and facilitate the establishment
of trust. However, at the proper time, the therapist, a modern
psychoanalyst, began "feeding" back to the patient small doses of
the aggression the patient was expressing in an indirect manner.
At this phase of therapy, the patient's posture of indifference was
breaking down. He had begun to come out of his isolation, only to
get involved with a succession of dominating and sadistic women

who each left him in a rage. His own mother had treated him similarly, while his father had been a schizoid personality, also withdrawn and unable to model a healthy way of functioning. The patient had reached a point in therapy where the rage that he had internalized for so long had become mobilized.

Noting the gradual externalization of this rage—which the patient expressed toward the therapist by frequently forgetting his checks and making jokes about the therapist's greed and indifference—the therapist began to actively draw out the patient's aggression. The therapist knew that until he did so, the patient's rage would remain a barrier to further communication and analysis and might possibly destroy the relationship. One day as the patient lay on the couch in a sullen silence, the therapist asked, "What are you thinking?"

"I'm thinking I don't want to talk to you today."

"That's right, hold on to all your shit and let it fester inside you as usual," the therapist replied.

"Go to hell," the patient mumbled.

"Is that supposed to tell me off?"

"Fuck you," he said a bit more loudly.

"I'll bet you'd like to."

"You're sick."

"How can you say that to a warm, lovable guy like me?"

"Fuck you."

"You said that already."

The patient's face became pale and he was quite still for a moment. Then he suddenly spat out, "You disgust me. You really do. I wish you'd die! In fact, I'd like to kill you myself."

"Yeah, you'd probably enjoy killing me, sick as you are."

"That's right. That's right. I'm sick all right! Sick of you!" the patient exploded. "I'd like to torture you, that's what I'd like to do. Killing's too good for you. I'd like to cut off your arms and legs, saw them off with a dull saw. I'd like to saw off your balls. I'd like to saw off your nipples. I'd like to pull out your fingernails and toenails, one by one. I'd like to slowly gouge out your eyes.

You disgust me and sicken me! Don't tell me I'm sick! *You're* sick, you greedy, anal-retentive creep, you're sick!" He spent the rest of the session lambasting the therapist with the hostility that had been repressed since infancy. During the following session he cried for the first time in the seven years of his therapy.

Intervention 63

The Compulsive Masturbator and the Family Therapist

After the boy's parents divorced when he was 5 years old, he became very angry at his mother and she became very angry at him. The boy's four older sisters sided with the mother. Everywhere the boy turned there were females hovering over him, telling him what to do. And mainly what they were telling him was that he had to stop playing with himself. Every time the boy fondled his penis, his mother or one of his sisters would try to pull his hand away. He masturbated even more. They tried to shame him. He masturbated even more. Before long he was masturbating at school in his classes and at home in the living room while everybody was watching television. This situation continued until the boy was 10. At that point in time a family therapist was called in.

The beginning phase of family therapy is to establish a rapport with the patients. The therapist, a young man, met with the family as a whole and then with the family members separately. After the therapist established a rapport with the mother, he asked her if she would allow him to work with the boy privately. She agreed. In this way the therapist forged a bond with the boy, serving as his surrogate father. The boy had not seen his real father since the father had run off with another woman, leaving the boy to deal with his mother's rage.

The therapist decided to use paradoxical directives. He asked the boy how many times he masturbated each day, and the boy reported that he generally masturbated about four times a day. "I'm going to have to punish you," the therapist said to him in a friendly but firm manner. "It's for your own good, and it's for the good of the treatment. You may think the form of punishment I'm going to give you is a joke at first, but you'll see it's no joke. What I'm going to ask you to do is to masturbate twice as much. For the next week I want you to masturbate eight times a day."

The boy laughed. "Oh, yeah? That's great." He had long scraggly hair down to his shoulders and blue eyes that were sad and bitter even when he was smiling. "That's the kind of punishment I like."

Meanwhile, the therapist suggested to the mother and four sisters that for the next week they pay absolutely no attention to the boy when he masturbated. He was interested in robbing the boy of the shock value of his masturbation, which was one of its main rewards. He also suggested to each of the females, separately, that they might be upset if the boy actually got better. Here again he was using paradoxical directives—as he had with the boy—telling them to do the opposite of what he wanted them to do, turning their resistance into a positive tool. By asking the boy to do more of what he was already doing, he was setting up a situation in which the boy would masturbate less in order to defeat the therapist. Similarly, by telling the mother and sisters they would be upset if the boy improved, he was giving them the chance to make him wrong.

A week later the boy reported that he had not fulfilled his assignment. Instead of masturbating twice as much, he had tapered off toward the end of the week and masturbated less. "Since you goofed on your assignment, I'm going to have to increase your punishment," the therapist said. "This week I want you to masturbate ten times a day, instead of eight."

"I can't masturbate that often," the boy protested. "It's impossible."

"Do it," the therapist replied.

After several weeks of this the boy had stopped his public masturbation completely. The therapist continued to meet with members of the family for another year, conducting weekly group therapy sessions. In these sessions they were able to analyze their communications problems and see how each contributed to those problems; in addition, they came to understand the traumatic episodes from the past that had led to the problems. This follow-up analysis insured that the conflicts that had caused the original symptom—the boy's compulsive masturbation—were resolved.

Intervention 64

The Therapist Who Confronted
a Borderline Patient

A borderline patient had established a pattern in the four years he had been in therapy of quitting every so often and then starting again. He would start out each time with a wave of enthusiasm, always apologizing profusely for running away and promising that this time it was going to be different and that he would commit himself to therapy. He promised also that he was "off of drugs." However, within six months he would suggest increasing the frequency of his sessions or would in some other way show his appreciation for the therapy, marking his inevitable sudden departure.

After four years, the therapist decided to try another approach. His usual intervention when the patient decided on a leave of absence was to say, "If that's what you think you need, then so be it." This time when the patient began expressing undue appreciation about the therapy, the therapist let out a derisive chuckle.

"Why don't you cut the crap?"

"What do you mean?" the patient innocently replied.

"You know exactly what I mean. Whenever you start with the compliments, it means only one thing. You're ready to take off again." The therapist gave the patient a pointed look and the patient laughed. "You think it's funny? It's not. You think I don't know what's going on? You think I don't know you've been taking drugs again? Apparently you'd rather kill yourself with drugs than do the one thing that would get you out of your destructive pattern; being honest with me about what you're thinking and feeling. Well, I'm sorry, but this time I'm not going along with it. You're going to have to make a choice. Either you stay and tell me what you're thinking and feeling about me and the therapy— I mean what you're *really* thinking and feeling—or you can run again and keep on running."

"Are you saying you won't take me back?"

"Correct."

"That's not fair!"

The patient stayed. At first he was angry and called the therapist many names. Then he began to truly admire the therapist (no longer pretending as before). Then he began to be honest. The work of therapy moved briskly on.

Intervention 65

Working through the Passive-Feminine Resistance

"It's hard for me to open up to another man," the young man said to his older male therapist early on in the analysis. For a long time he refused to lie on the couch. "It feels submissive," he said. After a year he brought in a dream in which there was a strange man lying in bed with him. When his therapist interpreted that the strange man was both his father and the therapist, the patient answered that he found the interpretation farfetched. The therapist did not venture an interpretation about the patient's fear of his homosexual feelings toward the therapist, knowing he was not yet ready to hear it. For another year the patient kept the therapist at a distance, refusing to acknowledge any feelings or thoughts about the therapist. Partly this was a negative, narcissistic transference having to do with his paranoid position in regard to intimacy with any authority figure, male or female, and with people in general. It was also connected with his passive-feminine fear of homosexual feelings and, beneath that, the desperate need for his father's love and approval, which he had never gotten. While the patient kept the therapist at a distance, he also kept everybody else in his life at a distance. His relationships with women seldom lasted for more than one or two dates; his fear was of opening up to a woman, revealing the depths of his need, and being rejected. (His mother had thoroughly rejected him, once calling him "asinine.") His relationships with his male boss and colleagues were also full of ambivalence. Never was there any honest communication in any of his relationships. His capacity to open up in his life seemed to depend on his capacity to open up to his therapist, yet he continued to resist. As the third year of therapy rolled around, the patient grew increasingly uncomfortable during his sessions. He would frequently come late and would sometimes have nothing to talk about. He would fall asleep. He would speak in a monotone about trifles. He acknowledged he was avoiding but said he did not know what he was avoiding. "I know what you want me to say," he told the therapist sullenly. "You want me to say I'm avoiding talking about my negative feelings about you, or my sexual feelings, or whatever, but I don't want to give you that. I don't want to give you anything. You're just like my father. He always wanted me to be his pal, but I didn't want to. So I have some sexual fantasies about you, so what? What good will it do to talk about them? Tell me what good it will do?"

"Instead of my telling you what good it will do, why don't you tell me what harm it will do?" the therapist replied.

"If I tell you these fantasies, I'll feel weak and submissive and small and stupid. It's stupid and weak to have these kinds of fantasies. Yes, I know you say it's common to have these fantasies toward your therapist, and it doesn't mean you're homosexual. But I'm not sure I buy that. Maybe I'm afraid I'll find out I really am homosexual."

"All right. Suppose you feel weak and stupid and start to think you're a homosexual. Then what will happen?"

"Then you'll confirm that I'm weak and stupid and homosexual, and you'll feel superior."

The therapist then asked him the single most-asked question in a psychoanalyst's repertoire. "Who used to treat you that way in the past?"

The patient quickly replied, "My father. And my mother, too." This same question had to be repeated many times over the next year before the patient understood—not only intellectually but emotionally—that the therapist was really not going to behave as his parents had. As the patient was able to understand that, he flipped from a negative to a positive transference.

"Oh, my God. I love you so much!" he blurted out one day.

"That's a good feeling," the therapist replied.

"It feels so strange to love somebody this way, especially a man." He spoke in a young child's quivering voice, hugging himself, his formerly hardened, bitter eyes now full of tears. "There are so many strange feelings inside me. I never knew I had such feelings. Now I feel like . . . this is strange . . . like I want to hold you and kiss you. Oh, God, am I gay?"

"No, you're not gay. This is just a normal phase of psychoanalysis. You're doing fine."

"Thanks." He broke into the deep sobbing of an infant. "I need your love so much! I need it with all my heart! I need it, I need it!" He was experiencing the needs that were frustrated by his parents when he was two and they "abandoned" him to visit Europe for several months. It was one of his strongest fixation points. "This is so strange. I had no idea I had all these feelings inside me. All this time I've been abusing you, resisting these feelings. This is strange. . . ."

Gradually the therapist, through his empathetic prodding, helped the patient work through and understand the needs that had been frustrated by his parents, which had led to the formation of his narcissistic character.

Intervention 66

Success through Silence

A young woman patient went through a period, during her third year of therapy, in which she rejected all of her older female therapist's interpretations. Sometimes the patient would reply, "That's ridiculous" or "I can't accept that." At other times she would simply continue with her free associations as though she had not even heard the therapist.

The therapist was baffled. She had been giving the patient interpretations with some success; now the patient had apparently regressed back to an oral-narcissistic defensive posture. For a while the therapist reacted angrily to the patient's rejection of her interpretations. Each time the patient rebuffed her she felt wounded, as though the patient were saying her interpretations were worthless (her milk was worthless, her femininity worthless, her self worthless). In retaliation, the therapist began giving more interpretations, and the relationship fell into an impasse.

Her countertransference had been aroused. The youngest of five children, the therapist had never felt her opinions mattered in her family, and one of her unconscious reasons for becoming a therapist was to gratify her need to feel listened to. The patient's negative transference had plugged into this countertransference reaction. Upon discussing the situation with her supervisor, the therapist was able to understand what had happened. The patient had appeared to develop an object transference and seemed to listen to interpretations, while in actuality she was acting out an idealizing transference. By doing so, the patient hoped to gain the therapist's love and approval. However, as the therapist heaped more and more interpretations on the patient, they were experienced more and more as attacks. The patient had then retreated to a more obvious narcissistic shell and began expressing her resentment by rejecting all interpretations.

The therapist, on her supervisor's advice, remained largely silent for several sessions, speaking to the patient only if the patient asked for a response. Eventually the patient asked, "How come you've been so silent lately?" The therapist used the opportunity to explain to the patient what she thought had been happening. "Ah, yes," the patient said. "I knew I was feeling angry at you about something, but I didn't know why." The impasse was broken.

Intervention 67

The Therapist Who Told a Patient He Hated Her

At the beginning of treatment she was quite withdrawn, a 19-year-old with dull brown eyes, short brown hair, and an obese body clad in drab gray or black shirts and pants. She lived with her parents in Upper Manhattan and was the youngest of five children. Her early childhood, a thing of sadism, had left her full of a rage that had since become internalized. She spent her days sleeping and her nights eating junk food. She watched television all night long. Twice a week she came to her therapy sessions, which she claimed her parents had pushed her into. She did not work.

"This is stupid," she would say, lighting up a cigarette despite the therapist's rule against smoking during sessions. She puffed and puffed, blowing smoke toward him. "I don't know why I keep coming. I guess because my parents are paying for it, so I might as well." She sat upright in a chair, casting a contemptuous glance at the couch. "And don't ask me to lie down on that ersatz couch, because I'm not going to. I've never heard of anything so preposterous." She continually referred to the therapist's couch as "ersatz" because it was imitation leather.

"I wonder how come you smoke when I've explained my rule about smoking being deleterious to therapy," the therapist said.

"I haven't the slightest idea," she said, blowing more smoke at him.

"Would you like to know why?"

"Not really."

The therapist, even in the beginning phase, found himself wanting to get rid of her. Her father had actually done so, again and again, kicking her out of his big townhouse after she had "bad-mouthed" him, banishing her from his kingdom for periods of time, letting her back in when she feigned an apology. He had always favored her older sister, a sleek, honey-blond beauty, while heaping abuse on the patient. Everyone in the family was continually picking on her, particularly on her obesity, but the father was obsessed with the obesity, viewing it as an act of outright treason. Meanwhile her mother, another sleek beauty like the older sister, pitied the patient and advised her to "keep it up and you'll never find a man who'll want you."

The therapist, a man of about middle age with rosy cheeks and a slightly balding hairline, tried numerous interventions. Often he countered her extreme negativity with humor, playing a father-object opposite of her real father, whom she described as a grouch. "How many psychoanalysts does it take to change a light bulb?" he asked her one day. She glared at him. "One," he answered to his own question. "But first he has to analyze the resistance." She did not laugh. Sometimes he remained silent for a whole session. She would talk in small flurries of negativity interspered with her own silences. Sometimes he told her inspirational stories about people similar to her. She was not impressed.

After two years of this she went through a period of several months during which she said not a word. She would come in, usually late, and sit in the chair with her arms folded while she gazed down at the rug. Sometimes she would close her eyes and pretend to sleep. The therapist was enraged by her silence and had an impulse to either kick her out of therapy or strangle her. She had told him that her father had once tried to strangle her right before one of the occasions on which he had sent her packing. As the silent sessions continued, the therapist was able to analyze and get control of his countertransference. Finally, he decided to let her know how he felt.

"You know, I really hate you right now," he told her. "When you behave this way, I really hate you. I just wanted you to know that." He scowled at her. He was being demonstratively angry.

"I . . . I don't know what you want from me." She blinked and looked terrified.

"I want you to talk!" he yelled.

"So, I'll talk . . . ." She began to do so, in a small voice bordering on tears.

It was a turning point. Not long after that she began to lie on the couch. By giving her an emotional communication, feeding back to her the unconscious hatred she had been feeding him, he had showed her she mattered. He had also made her aware of her impact on him and indirectly had given her permission to express her own hatred, of which she was still unaware. The intervention also served to establish an object transference; he had become real to her, a person separate from her or her father. In addition, the experience was helpful to the therapist, for in allowing himself to objectively express his countertransference feelings, he released some frustration and was able to be more empathic.

During the next few years the patient began to say nasty things to the therapist. Until the turning point she had been primarily paranoid, projecting aggression onto her environment. Now she began to own more of her aggression and direct it at the therapist. She told him he was a creep, a wimp, a toad. She disparaged his skills as a therapist, put down his humanity, doubted his masculinity. And she acknowledged, grudgingly, her fantasies of wanting to devour him, vampirelike, while he slept. The deep rage that had simmered inside her for so many years bubbled to the surface and got spewed on him. He encouraged it.

"Why do you say such nice things to me?" he would ask after a typically vitriolic attack.

"Because you're a creep, like my father."

"A cute guy like me?"

"Creep! Creep! Creep!"

There was about their relationship during this middle phase the aura of a romantic entanglement, except that everything was verbalized. They explored every aspect of her feelings toward him and his reactions to these feelings, including her sexual impulses. There were frequent outpourings of anger, as in any such relationship, and also moments of tenderness. In between, everything was analyzed. As this process continued she began to understand the meaning of her obesity and her negativity. Her weight gradually declined. She began to date.

One day after seven years of therapy she began to laugh. She laughed and laughed.

"What are you laughing about?" he asked.

"I was just remembering that session when you went out of control and started raging at me." She laughed again, shaking her head. "You looked like one of those bulls that have been speared so many times they begin to charge anything in sight. I thought for sure you were going to assault me that day. You should have seen your face. It was so red. It's funny now to think of it." She laughed and pointed at him. "Don't you think it's funny?"

"Sure," the therapist smiled wryly. "Very funny. Very, very funny."

Intervention 68

The Gratifying Therapist

A man who had been in therapy with a male therapist for several years came to a place in his therapy where he could not go on. He would start each session by saying, "I have nothing to say today," then lie on the couch with his eyes shut as though to close off the forces of evil. "All I keep thinking is that I'm a jerk. I'm a jerk, I'm a jerk, I'm a jerk." He had just been rejected by a woman he had been seeing, something that happened to him frequently.

During this period his therapist tried standard analytic techniques without success. The situation persisted. In analyzing it to himself, the therapist understood that the patient had developed a negative transference. He had been the whipping-boy of his family. From the time of his infancy on, his father had often wondered out loud if the hospital had given him the wrong baby. Once, when he was about 7, his father had angrily asked him, "Why are you such a jerk?" His mother, a weak woman, backed up the father's perception and often teased the boy about his big ears, calling him "Mickey Mouse." His older sisters joined in the fun. Little wonder that he had such a problem with self-esteem. Now in his relationship with the therapist he had a great need for something positive. The therapist's neutrality seemed hostile and depriving to him, reminding him of his parents. He responded by shutting himself off and he was immune to analysis. The therapist, who was not classically rigid, decided that a little gratification was needed to resolve the resistance.

"Suppose I said I didn't think you were a jerk?" the therapist asked one day. "Suppose I said I admire you?"

Tears sprang into the patient's eyes. "I think that's what I've been wanting to hear. All my life I've been wanting somebody – somebody I respect – to say that to me. But I don't know if I believe it. Why would you admire me?"

"I admire your dedication to therapy. You've come every week without fail. Many people are too resistant to seek or accept help."

"That's true. I have been dedicated, haven't I?" He paused a moment, and then said, "I wish you'd say things like that more often." He proceeded to speak of his need to be admired and expressed thoughts about the therapist that he had previously held on to. At a later time, when the patient again sank into the resistance of hopelessness, the therapist had only to ask him, "Should I say something positive?" – and the patient came to life. This time he expressed negative feelings toward the therapist and toward his parents. The cycle would repeat itself in many variations over the next two years.

Generally, gratification is not encouraged by most schools of psychoanalysis and psychotherapy. It is felt that in order for most patients to improve, they must work through their conflicts and complexes and learn to accept themselves; gratification by a therapist will create a dependency that will undermine a patient's striving for independent self-acceptance. However, there are exceptions to all rules. In this instance, the therapist avoided creating a dependency through the way he worded the gratifying remark – "Suppose I said I didn't think you were a jerk?" He also avoided creating dependency later when the resistance reappeared, when instead of offering gratification he merely reminded the patient that his resistance had to do with the need for gratification, as was evident on the first occasion when the therapist had offered him some. This insight then led the patient to express his frustration and rage.

Intervention 69

The Patient Who Did Not Want to Dirty His Therapist

During the beginning phase, an analytic candidate's five-times-a-week analysis was characterized by the stereotypical nature of the material: he spoke endlessly and monotonously about his problems with his girlfriend. The therapist, a training analyst at a reputable psychoanalytic institute, was referred to only when the candidate wanted advice about the situation. One day, after several months, the situation changed.

"I found myself feeling anxious as I approached your office today," the candidate announced at the start of the session. "And this anxiety is very similar to what I usually feel toward my girlfriend. I'm not sure what it's about. Maybe I feel guilty. I remember thinking, for instance, that I hadn't taken a bath or changed my clothes before coming here today. And I often have those kinds of thoughts when I'm going to see my girlfriend, too. Oh, God. I think there's a lot of guilt inside me. It makes me think this analysis might go on indefinitely."

Something important had happened; the candidate had begun to see and admit that the therapist existed for him, and had thus crossed into the middle phase. He had also expressed, indirectly, that he feared the therapist would discover what the patient regarded as dirty within himself. The dirtiness stood for his unconscious aggression, which he was afraid might destroy him or the therapist. This aggression took the form of anal fantasies of dirtying the therapist–bringing him down to the candidate's level.

"You're afraid I might find out you want to dirty me," the therapist interpreted. "You want to dirty me, bring me down, as you once wanted to bring down your father–and still do. But at the same time you also admire me and want to protect me from this dirtiness. Hence you feel the analysis could go on indefinitely. You're caught up in this conflict between wanting to dirty me and wanting to protect me."

"That's exactly it," the candidate said, nodding emphatically. "You hit it right on the nose." The candidate then elaborated on the interpretation, comparing his feelings about the therapist and his father and talking about the fears that had kept his free association at such a superficial level for so long.

Intervention 70

The Reluctant Analysand

Often in working with narcissistic patients (particularly of the borderline variety), psychoanalysts are confronted with a great deal of resistance with respect to the patients lying on the couch. This resistance may last a few sessions or a few years, and sometimes when such a patient finally does lie on the couch, the event signals the start of the middle phase.

One such case concerned a young woman who had come out of an extremely abusive family background. Her mother had deserted her at birth and had lived in a nearby city, where she earned her living as a prostitute. Her father showed up when she was about 11 years old, and whisked her away to America. Until then she had lived with her grandparents. Her life with her father and stepmother was full of violence. The father took the attitude toward the patient that she was a willful brat who needed to be tamed. He frequently beat her severely, and on one occasion he rammed her head against the wall repeatedly until she fell unconscious. She became the scapegoat of the family, which included several siblings.

Understandably, when she came into therapy at the behest of a sympathetic teacher, she immediately suspected that her male therapist would try to control her and abuse her. For her part, she was determined that nobody, especially a male, would ever control or abuse her again—and that on the contrary, she would control and abuse them. These thoughts, however, were mostly unconscious. On the surface she presented a shy, sweet facade.

Her therapist, still a psychoanalytic trainee, was partly taken in by this sweet facade and was also moved by the stories she related about her father. He was moved all the more because she would tell these stories without any emotion, as though it had all happened to somebody else. Meanwhile, the therapist began from the outset to explain to her the purpose of her lying on the couch, and the first power struggle ensued.

"If you lie on the couch it's better for you and better for me," he told her in a soft, friendly voice.

"I see," she said and smiled sweetly, nodding her head.

"It's better for you because if you're lying down it is a more relaxed posture, and your not looking at me then frees you to explore yourself in more depth. Instead of having a superficial conversation with me, you're having a deep, meditative conversation with yourself."

"I understand," she said smiling again.

"And it's better for me because if I don't have to look directly at your eyes I can be more objective about you. That helps me to be a better therapist."

"Yes, that makes sense," she nodded.

"Also, if you can lie on the couch, not looking at me, while I sit in a chair behind you, it recreates the kind of situation that happens in childhood. It allows you to experience being vulnerable with somebody, as a child is vulnerable, and having that somebody accept you and understand you rather than take advantage of you or behave destructively toward you. It's important for you to have that experience." The therapist, anxious to prove to her that he was not like her father, often went further than he had to in his explanations. However, when he came to the end, the patient would always nod her head and smile and he would say, "So, would you like to try it?"

"Not really," she replied, smiling very sweetly.

Months went by. Then a year. Then two years. Then three years. During the course of this time she remained seated in a chair facing him, despite his frequent efforts to persuade her to lie on the couch. However, during this time she not only refused adamantly to lie on the couch, but also resisted him in so many other ways that he often became exasperated in working with her to the point of wanting to ask her to leave therapy. Her demeanor gradually changed from that of a sweet, shy girl to a teasing vixen. She became quite demanding. She constantly asked that he change appointments for her. Then she complained that therapy was not helping her and would call him on the phone day and night to cancel appointments. Then she complained of financial difficulties, asking to delay her payment of his fee. She was continually attempting to manipulate him and defeat him, and she would not entertain for a moment any of his interpretations.

On one occasion she smiled at him in a teasing way and asked if he would do her a favor.

"What is that?" he asked.

"I know you're not going to believe me, but I'm having financial trouble again. I have to pay my rent this week, and so I'd like to pay you next week, if that's all right."

"Do I have a choice?"

"Of course you have a choice. I can either pay you next week, or if that's not all right, I just won't come next week."

"That's some choice. That's not a favor, that's a manipulation. Either I let you pay me next week, or I don't get my money."

"Oh, Doctor, you always look at things in such a negative way."

"Tell me," he continued. "How much money are you putting into your Christmas Club account each paycheck?"

"I knew you were going to ask that. On my way here I was

thinking in my head about what you were going to say, and I knew you were going to say that."

"So you prepared in advance to defeat anything I would say to you."

"No, that's not it at all. Oh, my God. I can't say anything to you. Oh, my God."

And so it went. Her negative transference toward him was almost entirely acted out, never verbalized. He could not seem to make any real inroads into getting her to stop the acting out or to verbalize her feelings toward him, much less to lie on the couch.

Finally, in the third year, feeling constantly irritated and enraged at her, he began to take a different approach. No longer was he the friendly, nurturing father figure who was going to show her what love was about. Instead, he became increasingly silent and withdrawn, then caustic, making sarcastic remarks about her resistant behavior. Unconsciously, he wanted her to go away. But she stayed. When she spoke of therapy not helping her or of wanting to quit, he would say, "That would be fine with me. It would be a relief to get rid of you."

"Oh, Doctor, what a thing to say," she replied, teasingly.

In his supervision he spoke mainly about her. His supervisor, an older man, had been working with him for some time to get him to understand his masochism. "Your need for her approval has gotten in the way of your objectivity," he kept telling the therapist. "You're letting her manipulate you. With patients like her you've got to draw the line and be very firm about it." The therapist insisted that he had been drawing the line. However, he had been doing it in a reactive, angry way, rather than in a calm way, and the patient knew she was getting to him. "You've got to overcome these countertransference feelings and act in a firm, calm way to stop her treatment-destructive behavior," the supervisor said.

Things came to a head a short time later. She began canceling one session after another. Their relationship became a series of brief phone conversations in which she would tell him she was not coming and he would tell her that was fine. Finally, after she had missed four weeks, he told her that if she canceled another session she would have to find another therapist. He said it as calmly as he could.

Her face was pale, her gait hesitant, when she walked through the door. She sat gingerly on the chair, smiling squeamishly.

"Lie on the couch," he ordered, in a firm but calm voice.

"Why?"

"Because I said so."

"But. . . ."

"I said lie on the couch."

She did as she was told, complaining that it was silly. She did not lie all the way down, but sat up, her hands behind her head. That was good enough for the therapist.

"Now, tell me what you're thinking."

From that moment on the therapy relationship changed. She began to express more anger at her father. She began to talk, in retrospect, about what a difficult time she had been giving the therapist. She began to take more responsibility for her feelings.

The therapist had taken a long while to learn that the intervention he needed to use with her was that of commanding her to do as she was told. In working with borderline patients, very often the intervention that works best in the beginning is the one that replicates the relationship they experienced with their parents. They do not trust any other kind of relationship yet. So the therapist in effect gives them what they are asking for, and at the same time is careful to let them know that he is acting that way because that's what they need, not because he is hostile. As they are able to tolerate more positive feelings from him, the therapist changes his approach.

Intervention 71

Identification

The young woman had been stuck for several weeks. She spoke in a lifeless voice and lay so still on the couch one might think she were dead. "I'm hopeless," she muttered every now and then. "I'll never get better. I'm just hopeless." For a few years she had been having an affair with a married man. Now that affair had abruptly come to an end as the man had moved, with his wife, to another country.

"If you're hopeless, then I must be hopeless, too," her female therapist replied.

"Why's that?" The patient sighed.

"Because I'm the hopeless therapist who's not helping you get better."

"It's not your fault. You mean well. It's just that you couldn't possibly understand what I'm going through."

"Why's that?"

"Well, I'm sure you never had an affair with a married man. You're too smart for that."

"Actually, I did have an affair with a married man, and it was when I was just about your age, too."

"Really?"

"Really. And I *do* know just how you feel."

The patient began to talk about her pain and the impasse was broken. Through the use of mirroring and identification, the therapist had demonstrated her empathy and understanding for the patient in a way her mother never had (her mother being an "I-told-you-so!" kind of person). Interventions involving the use of identification are helpful with a variety of patients and situations.

Intervention 72

The Feminist Patient
and the Nonfeminist Therapist

"I specifically asked for a woman therapist because I don't trust men," she told her therapist at the initial interview. "And, as a feminist, I have feelings about the way women are victimized by men that I don't think a male therapist would understand." This statement set the tone for the beginning phase of her therapy. In order for her therapist, who was not a feminist, to work with her during this phase of treatment, the therapist had to remain silent and empathic. She was careful not to contradict the patient with respect to her feminism or her views about men. For a year the patient used most of her sessions to complain about her relationships with men and about how men in general persecute women. She never asked the therapist's views on the matter or inquired whether the therapist was a feminist. She simply assumed the therapist was in agreement with her.

The patient was a borderline personality with strong narcissistic tendencies. Upon analyzing to herself the patient's early childhood, the therapist realized that the patient's anger at men was a displacement of the primary source of her rage, her mother. The patient had a hostile and controlling mother who had not only stunted her daughter's development, particularly during the anal-rapprochement phase, but also intruded on her attempts to form a relationship with her father during the oedipal phase. Since the mother was the dominant figure in the household, and the father was a weak, passive man, the daughter was not able to turn to the father for help in her strivings for separation and independence from her mother. Hence, although she was enraged by her mother's domination and control, she could not acknowledge or express this rage to her mother for fear of losing the latter's love and approval; instead, she followed her mother's example and developed a contemptuous attitude toward her father and toward men in general. Later, as an adult, her banding together with other women under the umbrella of feminism represented a symbolic extension of her alliance with her mother against her father.

During the first year of therapy the patient protected the therapist from her rage just as she had protected her mother. She needed the therapist to be in agreement with her—that is, she had formed a narcissistic transference in which the therapist was regarded not as a separate being with separate thoughts and feelings, but as an extension of herself, an alter ego with similar thoughts and feelings. Then, after the first year, things slowly began to change. The rage began to seep out in indirect ways, primarily through a subtle defiance. She refused to lie on the couch, continually came five or ten minutes late, and would not talk about her childhood, though the therapist had gently tried to lead her in that direction on occasion. Nor would she ever analyze her resistance.

"I'm sorry, but I just don't believe in psychoanalysis," she would say in a rather strident tone, gloating at the therapist. Her rimless glasses gave her an aura of intelligence and her short, curly hair accentuated that aura. "First of all, I think everybody knows that Freud was a sexist and a woman hater and his views on women are misogynistic. Secondly, I think he was an obsessive-compulsive who overanalyzed everything to death. I don't want to go around analyzing everything. It's boring." The therapist did not press her.

The second year went on in this vein. By the end of that year, the patient had begun to complain that the therapy was not helping her. When the therapist asked why, the patient replied that she did not think the therapist was the right kind of therapist: she was too Freudian. This was an important juncture, for it represented the first acknowledgment of the therapist's separateness. At the same time, the patient was also expressing more and more anger about her mother. It was here that the middle phase began, and the patient was able to start to look at and study her own behavior.

"What makes you think I'm a Freudian?" the therapist asked, utilizing an inquiring approach.

"Well, you keep wanting me to lie on the couch and you keep wanting me to analyze everything. Isn't that Freudian?"

"I use psychoanalytic techniques. Does that make me a Freudian? Does that mean I can't understand you?"

"I assume that if you use psychoanalytic techniques you must be a Freudian and that you must agree with his views about women."

"You're making a lot of assumptions about me, aren't you?"

"Are you saying you don't agree with Freud's views?"

"That's beside the point. The point is that you've made the assumption that I'm a Freudian, and are acting on that assumption by distancing me in different ways and pulling out of therapy without even exploring the matter with me. It seems to me that you're doing just what you accuse me of doing—you're being biased toward me. You've put me into a box, labeled me, and dismissed me as a human being."

The therapist and patient had many heated discussions around this issue throughout the third year and into the fourth. As they did so, they became more emotionally involved. The patient's ambivalence came to the surface, and she flipped back and forth from hating to admiring the therapist. At the end of one of her sessions she said, "You know, even though you're a Freudian dupe, you make sense sometimes." At the end of another she said, "You're the only woman I've ever met who's a male chauvinist pig." As the patient understood that she could express negative feelings toward the therapist without being punished or being made to feel guilty about it (as her mother had done), she began to work through the transference feelings and hated the therapist less and her mother more. At the same time, as she took more responsibility for her aggression, she realized that in her relationships with men she was more a victimizer than a victim. "I'm so sure men are going to victimize me that I do it to them first," she said.

Throughout the middle phase the intervention of choice was the inquiry method. This patient loved to use her intellect and loved to debate and to hash things out with the therapist (the underlying motive being to defeat her mother). The therapist recognized this trait and used it to the advantage of the therapy. In this sense each patient dictates the kind of intervention best suited to his or her character, and the wise therapist exploits a patient's traits and tendencies to the advantage of therapeutic progress.

This patient and therapist worked together for several more years and terminated successfully.

Intervention 73

The Therapist Who Videotaped
a Session

In the third year of therapy, a young man said he did not understand why women kept running away from him. "Do you think I'm angry?" he asked his female therapist. Before she could answer, he replied, "I don't think I'm angry."

For years women had been making hasty exits from his life. For years he had been rationalizing that they did so because of their problems with intimacy. For years he had been telling people he was not angry.

The therapist, having read an article about a therapist who was using video recordings of sessions, decided to try out this intervention. She asked the patient if he would mind having one of his sessions videotaped and he said he would not. "What have I got to lose?" The therapist borrowed some equipment from a colleague and taped the very next session, in which he ranted and raved about women who took advantage of him and then left him.

"Oh, my God," he said when he saw himself.

"What?" the therapist asked.

"I look . . . so fierce. Look at my eyes. Look at the way my mouth turns down on one side. Oh, my God. I never knew I looked like that. I look like an angry, uptight jerk." He shook his head, turning to the therapist for reassurance. She nodded. "Don't I look angry?" he asked.

"Yes, you look pretty angry."

"But I don't feel angry."

"I know."

"Why don't I feel angry?"

"That's what we have to understand."

"Oh my God," he said, staring at himself on television. "It's really amazing. I never knew I looked so angry. No wonder women are repelled by me. I can't stand it. I can't stand looking at my eyes. Turn it off. All right? I think I get the message. I think I get the message loud and clear."

Intervention 74

The Patient Who Feared Humiliation

A thin and gawky male patient told his male therapist he was afraid of opening up to him out of a fear of being humiliated. This fear of humiliation caused him to resist in various ways. For a time there were many silences, and the therapist interpreted that the patient regarded him as his teasing mother. Later, when the therapist laughed at something he said, the patient began to talk about quitting therapy, and the therapist interpreted that the patient regarded him as his older brothers, who had laughed at him and ridiculed him. At another point in the therapy, the patient's fear of humiliation also contained an aspect of physical fear, which was manifested in his not wanting to lie on the couch. The therapist interpreted that the patient now regarded him as his father, who had been physically abusive. On still another point he became proudly distant to the therapist, a compensation for the shame he had felt at having been made the butt of his schoolmates' jokes. Once again the therapist's interpretation managed to advance therapeutic progress.

During each of these instances, the therapist's most frequent intervention was the question, "Toward whom did you feel this way in the past?" This question is one of the most common in psychoanalytic practice. By having the patient trace his feelings of fear to his past, the therapist enabled the patient to understand his present response to him on both an intellectual and an emotional level.

Intervention 75

The Patient Who Wanted to Reject Her Therapist

She was a bright and pretty woman who had been abandoned by her real father soon after she was born and was abused by her stepfather from the age of three on. As an adult she suffered from depression. She had found, however, that her depression would lift for a while if she seduced and abandoned a man. Her pattern was to get involved with a particular kind of man, a man who had a problem such as alcoholism, but who at the same time had some degree of grandiosity. For about a year she would do everything this man wanted of her; she would rescue him from alcoholism, fulfill him sexually, and support his grandiosity. Then, suddenly, she would pull away and abandon him, leaving him shattered.

Naturally, the same pattern emerged in her relationship with her male therapist, a man slightly younger than she. For about a year she was the most obedient of patients. She was everything he could ever ask for in a patient: she paid a high fee, came on time, listened attentively to his every interpretation, brought in numerous dreams, and heaped him with compliments about his therapeutic brilliance, his sensitivity, his wisdom, and his integrity. The therapist knew something was up.

One day as she spoke of her pattern with men, he said, "It

seems your pattern is to seduce and abandon all the men in your life. You ingratiate yourself with them until they're hooked, and then you dump them, right?"

"That's basically it," she said, with a somewhat self-satisfied smile. "Although I don't think it's quite that simple."

"What I'm wondering," the therapist said, "is when you're going to dump me."

"Why would I do that?"

"I'm a man, am I not?"

"Yes, but this is different. You're my therapist. Why would I want to dump you?"

"You'll find a reason."

From then on the therapist kept asking her, from time to time, if she had found a reason to dump him yet. At first she would chuckle at this question, but when he had repeated it several times she began to react testily. "I'm beginning to think maybe you *want* me to dump you," she retorted.

"What I want," he said, "is for you to be aware of your pattern with men so that you can verbalize it rather than act it out this time."

"I'm sorry, but I don't agree with you. I don't think of you as a man. I think of you as a therapist."

"You don't think of me as a man? Thanks a lot."

The therapist was trying to provoke her. His repeated question as to when she would dump him, and his sarcastic remark, "You don't think of me as a man? Thanks a lot," were designed to confront her anger at her father and stepfather, at men, and—through the transference—at the therapist. He understood that unless he engaged her on a verbal level and provoked her into expressing this desire to dump him (drawing it up from the unconscious), she might indeed do just that. Like most hysterical-borderline patients, her aggression was largely unconscious, the awareness of which was defended against through the mechanisms of denial, reaction-formation, and projection.

"It looks like I'm going to be moving to Baltimore," she said a few months later. "I've been offered a job there that means a big promotion and raise in salary. I know you're probably going to think I'm dumping you, but it's not that. It's just a matter of economics. I hope you'll understand and be happy for me. But I'm afraid you'll take it personally." She had a grin on her face.

The therapist felt anxiety well up inside him and fought off the impulse to say something counterrejecting. He let her go on for a while, until he regained his composure. Then he asked, "You say you're not dumping me, right? In that case, if I could propose a way you could move to Baltimore and still be in therapy with me, would you be interested?"

"Well . . . sure . . . I guess." The smile faded. "But how could that be?"

"What I would propose is something that's being increasingly done nowadays—telephone therapy. You can continue your weekly sessions on the telephone. What I'd suggest is that you get yourself a speakerphone so that you don't have to hold the phone against your ear for fifty minutes. Then you can lie on a couch with the speaker behind you and it'll be just about the same as being in my office." The therapist's tone of voice mimicked the elated tone with which the patient had presented him with her news. In this way he was mirroring for her the way she conveyed aggression.

"Actually, it doesn't sound like a good idea. I hate telephones. No, I wouldn't do that."

"All right, suppose I come to Baltimore and see you there? I have a colleague there, and I'm sure he'd let me rent his office."

"You'd do that?"

"I might." The therapist was not really about to do that; he merely wished to explore her responses. "How about that idea?"

"I couldn't ask you to do that."

"You're not asking me. I'm proposing to do it of my own volition."

"I just think it would be better for me to start fresh with another therapist in Baltimore."

"Then it seems you *are* dumping me."

The patient was silent. "All right. I suppose I am."

"In that case, I think you ought to delay the move to Baltimore for a week or so to give us time to explore what's going on between us. I think it's important for your therapy to take a look at this. In fact, it may be a turning point. Would you be willing to delay your move for a few weeks in order to explore this issue?"

"That's ridiculous. Why should I do that?" the patient angrily replied.

"Because you care about your therapy."

"I'm not sure I care *that* much."

"Because you care about me."

The patient laughed incredulously. "I'm sorry, but I think that's funny."

"You mean you don't care about me?" The therapist acted surprised.

"I'm afraid not."

"In fact, you can't wait to get rid of me."

"I don't know if I'd put it that strongly."

"How would you put it?"

"Well, I guess I must be angry at you."

"You guess?" He looked at her sternly. "You're dumping me just like you've dumped every other man in your life. It's like a broken record already. When is it going to stop?" He was deliberately lecturing her.

The patient finally agreed to delay her move for a few weeks, and in the ensuing struggle she became acquainted with the feelings that underlay her pattern. She realized she did not really want to move and confessed that she was not really going to get a raise in salary at the new position. The therapist's repeated interpretation had finally reached her.

Intervention 76

The Primal Scream

"I feel like screaming," he said.

"How come?" his female therapist replied.

"Because I'm angry."

"What are you angry about?"

"I don't know. I just know I feel like screaming."

The patient, a man in his early twenties, had read about a form of "primal scream therapy" and had been asking his therapist, a psychoanalyst, to let him try it during his sessions. At first the therapist had resisted his requests to scream. She felt that his desire to do so was a resistance to the analytic process—a resistance to free association, to verbalizing his feelings, and to analyzing his resistance. However, as time went by she began to realize that he could not verbalize certain feelings because they harkened back to the early oral stage, a stage preceding the capacity for verbalization. The patient could not verbalize his rage from this period because it was beyond verbalization. This rage was infantile and deep as time itself.

The patient had been in therapy for several years and had been, for the most part, extremely passive. He had worked through most of his oedipal and anal issues and had now reached the oral ones. His mother had died when he was 1 year old, and he had become fixated at that state, stuck in a stage of incomplete mourning. His extreme passivity was a result of defending against the rage he felt toward his mother for dying and thus abandoning him, a rage he could not put into words or understand in an adult way. He also used the defense of ego-splitting; a part of him recognized his mother's death, but another unconscious part still awaited her return. His desire to scream stemmed from the gradual emergence of this rage during the course of the therapy, an emergence that he could feel inside his chest but could not understand verbally.

"After thinking it over," the therapist said to him one day, "I've decided that perhaps it would be beneficial for you to scream."

"Really?" The patient was at first surprised at the therapist's change of mind. "Are you sure?"

"I'm sure if you're sure."

"I'm very sure."

The patient proceeded to turn around on the couch, at the therapist's request, and scream into the pillow. He screamed for a few minutes, then stopped and reported that his headache had gone away. The next session he screamed for about five minutes. Again he reported that his headache had vanished. For several months he screamed for 5 or 10 minutes each session. At first his screams were wordless. Then he would scream, "Mommy, Mommy, Mommy!" Then he screamed, "I hate you! I hate you! I hate you! Why did you leave me, Mommy? Why? I hate you with every cell in my body! I can't stand you! Why? Why? Why?" His screams changed in texture during this period. In the beginning they were rather shallow and forced, but by the end they were deep and rasping like an infant's. Also, by the end he had started to sob. He would scream for only a short time and then cry until he was exhausted.

After a time, the patient himself decided he had had enough. "I don't think I'll scream today," he told the therapist.

"Why not?"

"I feel like I need to talk about it now."

"All right. I think that's a good idea."

The next year was devoted to processing his preverbal experiences.

Intervention 77

The Shifting Tides of Transference and Resistance

In her first year of analysis a middle-aged women who was married and had two children experienced a great deal of difficulty talking about her romantic longings for her male therapist—longings that had become apparent in her dreams. She felt that if she acknowledged such feelings about her therapist, it meant she was not happily married; this idea frightened her because she was quite dependent on her husband and harbored unconscious hostility toward him. The therapist patiently explained to her that it was normal for patients to dream of and have romantic fantasies about their therapists. But for a time she regressed, retreating into a shell of stubbornness. It was only after the therapist had repeated to her again and again that it was normal and that it would be beneficial for her to acknowledge her romantic and sexual feelings about the therapist that she began to come out of the shell, to face up to her positive feelings, and to admit to herself and the therapist that there were problems in her marriage.

Later, however, a new regression set in when the therapist began to interpret her negative feelings toward him. The patient became more silent during her sessions and developed severe gastritis. When the therapist suggested her gastritis was a somatic expression of her anger at him, the patient at first answered, "Don't be ridiculous." Again, the therapist had to repeat these interpretations many times, in many different contexts, before the patient began to take responsibility for her anger and to relate it to the primary figures in her past.

By the third year, the patient had once again regressed. This time it stemmed from the emergence of the patient's homosexual feelings. She had suddenly gotten in touch with thoughts and fantasies about other women, thoughts and fantasies she had denied until then. When the therapist interpreted them as homosexual, she again retorted, "Don't be ridiculous." Once again, it took a period of months for the working-through process to take effect. As it did so, the woman's outside life began to improve.

Her relationships with her husband and children became more genuine and she developed a variety of interests. In addition, she had changed from a rather passive woman to one who was able to assert herself in all aspects of her life.

Intervention 78

The Patient Who Wanted to Use Her Therapist's Telephone

She was one of those oral types who had always been given everything she wanted by her mother and now considered the world a big breast that should always be available to her. Whenever somebody in her life—her boyfriend, her boss, a friend—did not give her what she wanted or did not behave in a way she regarded as fair, she would become enraged. Her female therapist had attempted to analyze her oral demandingness and its consequences in her life, and the patient understood on an intellectual level. Yet the pattern of demandingness, rage, and vindictiveness toward her "persecutors" persisted.

One day after several years of therapy she rushed into her therapist's office and said in a presumptuous manner, "I'm going to use your telephone, okay?"

"Suppose I said it wasn't okay?" the therapist answered.

"I just want to make a quick call," the patient snapped. "It's no big deal."

"Suppose I say you can't make the call? Then what?"

"Never mind."

The patient plopped onto the couch and retreated into a sullen silence. The therapist waited a few minutes and then asked what she was thinking. The patient verbally attacked the therapist, calling her petty, snotty, and arrogant. "I feel like walking out of here!" she said. "I don't think I was asking so much. I really don't!"

"The problem was, you weren't asking. You were demanding," the therapist replied. She pointed out that the patient's tone of voice and manner of "asking" had set up the situation so that only an affirmative answer would be acceptable. "When I answered in the negative, your attitude was that there was something wrong with me. And I think this is what happens to you in your outside relationships. You don't respect other people's feelings. If they don't give you what you want—if they don't see things your way—they're wrong, bad, petty, et cetera." The therapist paused to let it sink in. "What do you think?" she asked after a while.

"Fuck you. I'm tired of always being blamed for everything!"

At the session's end the patient was still angry. However, a week later she lay on the couch and said, "I've been thinking about our last session. I don't know . . . maybe I *do* set it up some way for people to reject me. I had an argument with my boss this week. . . ."

Intervention 79

The Hail-Fellow-Well-Met

He did not really think he had any problems to speak of. He was an exceptionally successful attorney, had a wide social circle, and was beloved in his family. He was one of those hail-fellow-well-met types, full of enthusiasm, generosity, and wit. Negative emotions and thoughts were strangers to him. His analysis became an extension of his social life. He was an enthusiastic, generous, and entertaining patient who told fascinating stories and found his analyst's interpretations "on the mark," and he was never pained by anything in or out of analysis. He admired, flattered, and proclaimed the virtues of his analyst to all around, recruiting many new patients. He repeatedly invited the analyst to all parties, even though the analyst always declined, and was convinced he was the analyst's favorite patient. He reacted to the analyst as he did to everyone in his life, by trying to charm.

For more than a year the analyst could seem to make no real headway with this patient. He understood that in reality the patient was a manic-depressive stuck in the manic mode, always on the run from depression. The only signal of the depression that underlay his chronic enthusiasm was a sleep disorder. He had become addicted to sleeping tablets, which was what had brought him to analysis in the first place. The breakthrough in the patient's depression came as the result of an ongoing interpretation of his dreams.

A recurring theme in his dreams had him at a party, a meeting, a luncheon, at which nobody paid attention to him. The analyst repeatedly interpreted that the patient had developed a false self; he needed constantly to charm everybody, fearful that if he did not they would see through and disapprove of him. In his dreams this is precisely what did happen. "Your enthusiasm, your feeling of being everybody's favorite, of always being happy, is a myth you've created to defend against your depression and low self-esteem," the analyst said. "In reality you're not everybody's favorite, but they let you go on believing it in order not to offend you." At first the patient was unfazed by these interpretations. He thought they were brilliant but he could not feel his depression. After months of work, his unreal enthusiasm became ego–alien and he began acknowledging to himself, to his analyst, and then to others, the anger and sadness inside him. Until then he had maintained the same generalized transference onto everybody. Now his transference became more particular. The analyst became his seductive and rejecting mother, then his competitive father, then his spiteful younger sister. As the working-through process continued, the patient's life outside the therapy office began to change. His enthusiasm and charm took on a more realistic quality. He became aware that people were humoring him rather than being genuinely interested, and he became more restrained.

"What a relief to know I don't always have to be on," he said at the end of a productive session. "I don't always have to be the life of the party. I can just be myself. And the irony of it is, being myself is more interesting anyway, and less off-putting."

Intervention 80

The Loneliness of Life

"Life is so lonely," she said in a whimper. She said it again and again; it was the main theme of her therapy. Here she was, a beautiful young model and actress, men swarming around her, friends regaling her, and yet she was lonely. Where had this loneliness begun? Her therapy process was a step-by-step uncovering of its source.

Her middle-aged male therapist at first looked for the wellsprings of her loneliness in her manner of relating to her boyfriend. "He doesn't really care about me," was her constant complaint. "All he cares about is sex. I never feel as though he opens up to me." The first year of therapy was an ongoing complaint about her boyfriend's detachment, which always left her feeling lonely. Yet, the therapist noted, she did not really open up to him either. Nor did she open up to the therapist. Indeed, she was quite narcissistic, and during the beginning phase she needed him to be her alter ego, an entity that always saw things as she did. The therapist found himself feeling lonely during her sessions, for he could not be his real self with her but had to be an extension of her. This in turn provided him with information about what her relationship with her parents and

siblings had been like. And perhaps because she was the youngest, she had become the ultimate target of this kind of narcissistic
relationship. Was that the source?

Toward the middle of the second year of therapy she began
getting in touch with a lot of sadness and anger. The sadness and
anger came out in the transference situation – she began talking
about moving away from New York, back to California. She took
frequent vacations and was sick much of the time. When the
therapist interpreted that all these were forms of resistance and
represented the acting out or somatizing of her feelings of sadness and anger, she grew red in the face and angry at her family.
"My mother and father were always working in the restaurant,
and my brother and sisters always did things together. I was
always alone." She remembered her sisters taking her to nursery
school and back, caring for her until her parents returned home
from work late at night. "I feel so angry!" she said, pounding the
couch. "But I don't want to blame my parents. They did the best
they could." She remembered then that whenever she had complained to her parents, they had always answered that they were
doing the best they could; this memory brought up another well
of anger and another urge to pound the couch. Was this the
source of her loneliness?

A few months later she remembered how sadistic her older
sister had been toward her. The sister had resented having to be
a baby-sitter for her younger sister, and as soon as the parents
left she would address her in a surly voice, as though she were
the world's biggest nuisance, refuse to feed her when she wanted
to be fed, and would abandon her for long periods of time. "I hate
her," the patient said, pounding the couch again and crying like a
child. Was this the source?

Still later she would come to her session full of anger and a
deeper kind of sadness. Sometimes she would just rage and cry
for whole sessions. And then another memory presented itself, a
vague one. She remembered at about the age of 1½ or 2, being
left alone in her crib; she had become so angry she tried to climb

out and fell to the floor. Still nobody came. Then when she crawled into the kitchen, her sister scolded her and carried her roughly back to the crib. Her protests were to no avail. "I could hear my older sisters and brother laughing and playing in the other rooms, and I was always alone," she sobbed. "It seems I was all alone from the very beginning." Her mother, tired from raising the other children, had been in a hurry to wean the last child and return to the restaurant to help her husband. This early weaning no doubt also contributed to the feeling of abandonment and loneliness, as well as to her problems with bulimia.

As the patient waded through the labyrinth of her layers of fixations, her life on the outside began to change, as well as her relationship with the therapist. She no longer tried to get the people around her to "feed" her, understanding that the loneliness had to be resolved within herself. Her bond to the therapist improved to the extent that she became analyzable. She was able to tolerate more and more interpretative material.

"I feel as if I'm ready to stop therapy," she said after the fifth year. "I've learned so much from you. I think I can do it on my own now. I don't feel lonely anymore. What do you think?"

"I agree," the therapist said.

"What do we do now?"

"Now we begin the termination phase."

"The termination *phase?* That sounds heavy."

"Sometimes it is."

"Oh, God." She sighed. "Does this process ever end?"

Part Three

INTERVENTIONS OF THE TERMINATION PHASE

Intervention 81

A Little Less Loneliness

Psychoanalytic psychotherapy does not merely strive to remove symptoms or help a patient through a crisis; its goal is to bring about a change of character. That is why it takes so long. The pathological defenses—which most often represent self-defeating character flaws—are studied and to some extent dismantled. The fixations that lie beneath the defenses are resolved by way of analysis, catharsis, and working through. A new, healthier mode of being is learned as the transference relationship is analyzed and the real relationship develops. It is when this real relationship becomes stable that the termination phase is imminent.

In five years of hard work, the lonely patient described in the preceding intervention had truly undergone a change. In the beginning she had been quite narcissistic, unable to form a satisfactory relationship with anybody because of a deep-seated fear of abandonment and of being abused and destroyed by deceptive communication. She had defended herself through denial and projection. In her relationships she had attempted to manipulate through the induction of guilt. She would invariably choose men who were not really available—either they were married or too attached to their mothers or latent homosexuals.

She projected her aggression onto the men, viewing them as persecutors who enjoyed keeping her at an emotional distance while using her sexually. She denied her own aggressive feelings, and for the most part they became somatized. She would develop one illness after another—chronic hepatitis, tapeworms, infected ovaries, menstruation problems—while avoiding the anger that welled inside her. And, of course, there was her on-again off-again struggle with bulimia, her inability to assert herself in her acting career, and a general difficulty in relaxing and in being spontaneous.

As the therapy progressed all of these problems gradually waned. When termination was first broached, she had established a relationship with an available man and had learned how to trust and how to communicate honestly about her feelings; she had taken charge of her career (giving less power to agents and her manager); had not had any illnesses for over a year or been bulimic for two years; and she was generally more relaxed and spontaneous.

After her therapist agreed to termination, there came the usual pretermination regression. She abruptly developed another illness, a form of mononucleosis, which dragged on for more than a month. However, by this time she was aware of the link between emotional stress and her illnesses.

"I guess I'm afraid to terminate," she said, looking a bit apologetically at the therapist. At his request she had begun to sit up during the termination phase. This was done in order to normalize the relationship and "wean" her from the couch.

"What are you feeling?" the therapist asked.

"I feel as though you're trying to get rid of me, although I know that's not really true. It's my parents leaving me with my older sister all over again. Will I be able to deal with the older sisters of the world without you? Will I start feeling lonely again? Help! I'm scared."

"But now you're able to verbalize all this. A few years ago you weren't even aware of any of this."

During the termination phase the therapist provided mainly supportive therapy. This intervention was used to combat the regression that had set in and to strengthen her natural inclination toward independence, which had first been stifled during the separation–individuation phase of childhood. He also had to analyze and overcome his own resistance to letting the patient go. For a month he helped her work through the feelings of abandonment by having her talk about them. She was quite able to take the initiative in this regard and did not need much help. The more she talked, the more the illness waned. The next item on the agenda was what, if any, relationship she and the therapist would have after therapy. She wondered if they could be friends.

"Not for a while. It's important for you to learn to stand on your own feet now," he told her. "Your desire to be friends with me, while partly coming from a genuine base, may also be a way of clinging to me."

"It just seems too strange, after all we've been through together, to just go cold turkey, so to speak. I mean, this has probably been the most intimate relationship I've ever had. And now it has to just end. It's a bit hard to swallow."

Another month was spent on helping her to make peace with the fact that it was best to break off the relationship completely. The therapist no longer spoke to her in an authoritarian manner, but more like a good, old friend. In a warm, understanding manner he told her she could continue to see him as a patient if she needed a follow-up visit, and she could telephone or write him. But because of the special nature of the relationship, they would probably never be friends in the ordinary sense. She might find that hard to understand now, but later she would know just what he meant. "You've established a network of friends now, and you'll be all right," he told her.

"I feel almost like I did when I left home to go to college," she remarked.

"It's very similar," the therapist replied, sitting back in his chair, arms around his head. "Just think of this as another separation from Mom and Dad. Think of me as your Therapeutic Godfather." He grinned like a cherub.

"That sounds good." She laughed, then became thoughtful. "I just hope I won't miss you when I stop seeing you."

"You might miss me for a while, but then you'll be fine."

"I *know* I'll miss you."

"I'll miss you too."

They smiled at each other. They had established genuine feelings for each other that would endure despite the cessation of their relationship.

They set a date for termination. This was done in order to put a definite time frame onto the termination procedure; otherwise it might have lingered on. It was also a way of forcing them to deal with all the issues that needed to be dealt with. When the last session came to an end, the patient stood and smiled, holding out her arms.

"Could I have a good-bye hug?"

The therapist had constantly refused her hugs. Now he gladly acquiesced. A hug at this point was not only acceptable, but *de rigueur;* it was a symbol of their real relationship, as distinguished from the transference. To refuse the hug might have constituted a resistance to letting go, a method of frustrating the patient and keeping her under his sway. He hugged her for as long as she wanted. When she drew away, he did so as well.

"Good luck," she said, tears in her eyes.

"Good luck to you," he replied, and there were tears in his eyes as well. "Have a good life!"

Intervention 82

The Therapist Who Did Not Want
to Let Go

"I think maybe it's time for me to terminate," a male patient said to his female therapist.

"Let's talk about it," she replied.

She found herself feeling anxious as they spoke about it, and at first she thought the patient was arousing this anxiety in her because he was acting out the transference. He had just gotten married after having gone through a long erotic transference with the therapist in which he had often expressed the hope of marrying her. However, he had also spent a year working through the transference. The more she thought about it, the more she realized that the anxious feeling was her own subjective countertransference. The patient had become a substitute for the older brother who had always rejected her as a child, and his wanting to leave rekindled those early feelings of rejection. Once she had analyzed these feelings, she was able to come up with the right intervention.

"I think you're right," she told him the following session. "I think you *are* ready for termination."

"I am?"

"Yes. For sure, there's always more to work on, but at this

point in your life you've become quite actualized. You're happily married, you have a job you enjoy, and you haven't been drinking for seven years. I'd say you're ready to go if you want to."

"I do want to, but I hope I'm not deluding myself in some way, as I've done in the past."

"Well, let's take our time. We'll set up a termination schedule and take a few months to wind things down, just to make sure."

"That sounds great."

The therapist and patient worked together over the next few months, wrapping things up. Having overcome her own resistance to letting go, she was able to help him overcome his, by being steadfast in her support of his leaving therapy and establishing independence–which is, after all, the ultimate goal of all therapy. Once she was able to provide the correct intervention– supporting his desire to leave–the termination went smoothly. Sometimes it happens that way.

Intervention 83

The Therapist Who Revealed Himself

"You're divorced?" the patient asked, surprised.

"Oh, yes," the therapist said. "And I have a daughter about your age."

The two men looked at each other.

"A daughter my age? I can't believe it. How long have you been divorced?"

"Three years."

"That's amazing. All this time you've been going through a divorce and you never let on."

"How does that make you feel?"

"Well, in a way I feel hurt that you didn't trust me enough to tell me. But it's also comforting to know that you're human like me."

During the beginning and middle phases it is usually best for a therapist to remain a blank screen upon which patients may transfer primary figures from their past. This makes it easier to analyze such transferences, since any assumptions the patient then makes about the therapist are not based on actual facts but come from the patient's projections. However, during the termination phase the therapist begins to behave more and more genuinely with the patient in order to model a real relationship, with all its imperfections. In line with this, he begins to reveal more about himself. Such interventions help the patient to let go of any lingering tendencies to idealize the therapist, and to better make the distinction between the transference and real relationship.

Intervention 84

The Spontaneous Recovery

A 16-year-old high school student had sought help after the death of her mother. At the time she was having problems both at school and in her relationship with her father. Her mother's accidental death had left her in a state of depression from which she could not emerge, and her father was of no help.

"I don't know why I can't get over this," she kept saying to the therapist, an older male.

The therapist saw right off that what she needed was a real relationship with a father figure whom she could respect, one who was there for her empathically; who respected her feelings. After quickly establishing a rapport with her, he helped her discover that her poor academic performance was a reaction to her father's behavior after her mother's death. The father had immediately gotten involved with another woman and was not available to the daughter, who naturally needed to talk with him about the tragedy. Now, as she became aware of her anger at her father and its relationship to her schoolwork and responded to the mutual respect of the therapy relationship, a spontaneous growth set in. Seven months later she asked if she was ready for termination.

"Do you feel you're ready?" the therapist asked.

"Yes, I do. But what do you think?"

"It seems to me you're pretty much back on track. I don't see why we shouldn't begin to plan a termination date."

They arranged for a termination date that would coincide with the last week of school. In this instance a lengthy therapeutic relationship was not necessary, for the young woman was basically healthy and her depression was primarily situational. The therapist recognized that and responded with the proper intervention by letting her go when she felt ready to go, supporting her spontaneous recovery.

Intervention 85

Termination of a Schizophrenic

She had been in therapy for twenty-two years and did not want to leave, although her therapist felt she was quite ready to do so. She had to admit that all signs seemed to point toward termination, yet she resisted. She was happily married and had a job working for a museum, which she enjoyed, and had long ago given up her schizophrenic defense mechanisms of withdrawal, delusions of grandeur, and paranoid projections. It had been a long and often trying therapy relationship, and the present closeness between patient and therapist had not come without a struggle; therefore it was not easy to let go.

For the first eight years she sat facing the therapist, keeping him in her sight at all times. In the beginning he was treated as though he were some alien force that she had to be constantly on guard against lest he turn on her as other primary figures had done. After a few years of this he had been allowed to serve as a transitional object. Well into the eighth year she became faintly aware of anger at him and began forming an object transference.

The anger began gushing out in various ways for the next four years and was analyzed. Then for several more years an

erotic transference had set in and was analyzed while she lay on
the couch and increased the frequency of her sessions. Analysis
proceeded briskly and her world normalized.

After twenty-two years they had become friends, and the
patient used her sessions mainly to chat with him as she would
with any friend. However, when the therapist brought up termination, she grew quite pale.

"You know, I never even thought about terminating. And
now that you mention it, I feel scared," she said in a subdued
voice. "I guess I thought I'd continue with you until I die. Do we
really have to stop?"

"Yes, we do. But first we have to resolve your dependency."

She had become extraordinarily dependent on him, and
although this dependency had been necessary while she regressed and worked through infantile material, it was inappropriate under the present circumstances. His task now was to
resolve the dependency without causing a regression. He decided
to intervene by talking with her as a friend.

"You know, I hate to break up our relationship as much as
you do," he said. "I feel very close to you, and we've shared some
deep and personal things. But it's time for you to move on. I know
you feel as if I'm abandoning you, but those are the old transference feelings. We could go on this way for the rest of your life or
mine, but that would be robbing you of the growth you will derive
from cutting the cord completely and knowing you can do it
yourself. You can fool yourself into thinking you still need me for
this or for that, but it would be a lie and you'd be wasting your
money and jeopardizing your growth. Believe me, this is as hard
for me as for you. But we really must do it."

The therapist had to repeat these talks again and again,
then deal with the feelings they aroused—generally the anxiety
associated with separation. However, there was no regression on
the patient's part, only the anxiety and, for a time, a stubborn
refusal to deal with the issue. "I'll let you know when I'm ready to
terminate," she would reply, and go on to another subject.

Eventually she agreed to discuss a schedule of tapering-off sessions; then to set up such a schedule; and then, as the sessions tapered off, to let go of her sadness and anger at having to separate. Two years were spent on the termination phase.

She needed much reassurance during this period. Even during the last session she asked, for the tenth time, "If I have a crisis, can I still come back?"

"I'm always as near as the phone," the therapist repeated for the tenth time.

She called him once, a year later, to wish him a merry Christmas, reporting that all was well.

"I miss you, but you were right," she told him. "I do feel better about myself now that I'm completely independent of you."

Intervention 86

Termination as an Intervention of Last Resort

Ever since Freud, in his famous "Wolf Man" case, used a fixed termination date as a means to break an impasse, this intervention has been one of the accepted tools of the therapist's bag. A present-day therapist had a patient much like Freud's. This patient had been in therapy for four years and had made some progress. When he had first come to the therapist he had been living on unemployment insurance and was caught in an almost immobilizing depression. Therapy succeeded in getting him back to work and in alleviating the depression, but after a certain period no further progress could be made. For more than two years the patient kept insisting he was all right. He was primarily in a manic mode during this time and did not wish to stir up the old depression by delving into the conflicts that underlay his cyclical characterology. Yet he did not wish to terminate and never brought it up. He was content with the status quo. It was the therapist who finally brought up termination.

It was the session following his summer vacation and the start of a new "season" of therapy. "I just wanted to let you know that I've decided this will be your last year of therapy. No matter what progress you make or don't make, we'll be ending it next summer," the therapist announced.

"I don't believe you," the patient replied. He was a balding man with a paranoid substructure to his character who was always suspicious of everybody and everything. "I thought therapists weren't supposed to abandon patients?" He looked up from the couch, a slight skeptical smile in his eyes, and ran his hand over the dome of his head—one of his many nervous habits.

"Not in times of crisis. But since you seem to be doing all right and it appears we aren't making any progress, a termination seems in order."

"Then you really mean it?"

"Yes, I do."

It took a while before the patient understood that the therapist was not just bluffing. For weeks the patient joked with the therapist about it, not taking it seriously. When finally it did sink in, his depression returned. He began to talk about the things he had been avoiding. By the end of the year all kinds of new material had been discovered.

"Could we please extend the termination date?" the patient asked, glancing nervously back in the proximity of the therapist while stroking his dome. "I don't see what harm it would do to extend the date a bit."

"I guess we could extend it if you really feel motivated to continue."

"Of course I feel motivated."

They set a new termination date for the following December 31. However, when that date was reached, the patient again appealed for more time. Another termination date was set. Thus the termination phase became extended for three years. In this way, the therapist was able to shift the responsibility for therapeutic success onto the patient, helping him overcome his paranoid suspiciousness, his negative transference and resistance, and his fear of depression and the painful memories and feelings that lurked beneath.

"It seems we could keep extending the termination date forever," the patient said at the end of the final termination period.

"We could," the therapist said.

"You're pretty tricky, the way you keep me going."

"Yes, aren't I?"

The patient laughed and gave his dome an extra-long wipe.

Intervention 87

The Fetishist and the Father–Analyst

He had been a fetishist when he first entered therapy, and he became a fetishist once again when termination was discussed.

As a boy he was raised in a fatherless home, ministered to by his mother and grandmother, who were not tolerant of the boy's masculine strivings. To preserve his existence, which seemed threatened by the sexual animosity directed toward him, he developed a fetish–an attraction to and obsession with women's shoes. Later, during adolescence, he masturbated frequently while rubbing one of his mother's shoes against himself, the shoe being a symbolic reminder of his mother's phallic power. During the beginning phase of therapy, the therapist became a symbol of his fetish; the patient spoke frequently about his fetish, involving the therapist in the process. During the middle phase, the therapist served as a masculine alter ego, a father–analyst who could be there while the patient separated from his mother and grandmother and came to grips with the masculine strivings these two women had frustrated. Then, when termination was discussed and he was faced with separation from the therapist– who had by now become a friend and ally–he retreated once again into a shell of narcissism in which the therapist became his fetish. He began to talk a great deal about masturbation, as he had in the beginning.

To help him out of this pretermination regression, the therapist repeatedly interpreted the patient's fear of termination as a fear of disintegration. "You're afraid that without me you'll return to the state of being you were in before therapy, the state of isolation and coldness and detachment from others that began with your relationship with your mother and grandmother. But things are different now. You have people around you. And I'll always be with you; the experience of bonding you've had with me will always be a part of you. That fear of disintegration isn't a realistic fear now."

The patient listened to the therapist as though he were listening to a shoe. Then he told of his fantasy. "I was masturbating before I went to sleep last night. I fantasized that you were in my room. You were wearing my mother's red patent leather shoes."

The regression lasted another three months. By repeating the interpretation, the therapist was able to calm the patient's fears and bring him to a readiness for and acceptance of termination.

Intervention 88

The Therapist Who Moved
to Another City

"Before we start I need to inform you that I'm going to be moving
to another city at the end of the year," the female therapist told
the younger woman who had been her patient for four years.
"I've accepted a teaching position in Ohio. So, obviously that
means we only have a few more months to wrap things up." The
therapist paused to let the information sink in. "How do you feel
about what I've said?"

The patient, who sat facing the therapist, stared at her
mentor in shock. "I can't believe it. I don't want to believe it.
In the back of my mind I think perhaps you're testing me,
provoking me."

"No. It's not a test. It's true. I'm going to be leaving."

"What can I say? I'm stunned."

The patient left not knowing exactly how she felt, but
during the week she grew more and more angry. Due to the
masochistic aspect of her character, she imagined that the therapist had taken a sadistic delight in telling her this news (the
sadistic delight her brother had taken in teasing her when she
was a child). She was sure she had detected a smile on the

therapist's face, a smile of triumph. All week she thought about the therapist's smile, and she decided to counterreject her.

"I've decided to quit therapy," she informed the therapist the following week. "Since you're going to be leaving in a few months anyway, I don't feel there's any point in continuing with you. I think it would be more advantagous for me to begin with another therapist."

The therapist remained silent as the patient elaborated her reasons for quitting. She deliberately withheld comment until the patient asked for it, knowing that unasked-for comments in these situations were simply fodder for repudiation.

When the patient finally stopped to ask what the therapist thought, the latter replied, calmly and neutrally, "I can understand your thinking, and I agree that there might be some advantage in starting immediately with another therapist. But I also think it would be rash to quit today. I'd suggest that we at least take a few sessions to discuss it. How do you feel about that?"

"I don't like it."

The patient argued with the therapist about it, exclaiming at one point that she did not think the therapist would stay a few extra sessions for her when it was time for the move to Ohio. However, by the end of the session she relented, agreeing to come for three more sessions. During these sessions the therapist helped her to work through her anger and understand the transference. When the patient had worked through the anger, she was left with feelings of sadness associated with the therapist's abandonment (which rekindled feelings she had had about her mother). When they had worked through that, the patient experienced anxiety and expressed fears that she would never find another therapist to replace her.

The therapist took great care in finding another therapist for the patient and suggested that she begin seeing the new therapist a few weeks before their termination date. This last intervention insured a smooth transition from one therapist to another.

When they parted, the patient said, "I still feel sad to lose you, but I'll always remember the kind and caring way you ended the relationship with me."

Intervention 89

The Fat Patient
and the Paradoxical Therapist

The woman had been in therapy with her male therapist for seven years, and they had made a great deal of progress. She had overcome the depression that had brought her to therapy, and she had made advances in her career and in her personal relationships. However, whenever the therapist brought up the topic of termination, the patient always answered, "But I haven't lost weight yet." The therapist understood that she was using her obesity as a way to cling to him, just as it had once been a means of clinging to her mother. In order to break through the resistance, he decided to use a paradoxical intervention.

"I really think it's time for us to begin discussing termination," he said again.

"But I don't think I'm finished yet," she answered, as usual. "I still haven't lost the weight."

"You'll never lose the weight," he quickly retorted.

"Why do you say that?"

"Because in the seven years you've been in treatment with me you've constantly reported being on a diet and yet never lost a single pound. I think it's time we faced the fact that you're probably not capable of losing weight."

"You're just saying that to rile me up."

During the next six months the therapist continued this approach. Each time he brought up termination, he would deride the patient's ability to lose weight. Subsequently she began to lose a few pounds here and a few pounds there.

"I'm down to 158 pounds," she would report.

"It won't last," the therapist would reply.

The patient would laugh, saying she knew what the therapist was up to. But, nevertheless, she kept losing pounds. Within six months she was down to what she felt was her normal weight. In the process much anger and anxiety about her sexuality came to the surface. They worked on it.

"Now can we discuss termination?" the therapist asked.

"I'm . . . scared," the patient said.

"I know," the therapist said. "I know."

Intervention 90

The Patient Who Wanted a Certificate
of Mental Health

"The thing about therapy is you don't get anything tangible to show for it," the young man with a freckly face and anxious brown eyes said to his older male therapist. "I mean, if you graduate from college you get a diploma. If you go through a training program you get a certificate. I'd like to get a certificate for therapy. Then maybe it would seem more worthwhile."

"What kind of certificate?" the therapist asked.

"A certificate of mental health. You know, a piece of paper I could show people that would certify that I was mentally sound."

"All right. I'll tell you what. If you and I reach a point where we agree you've completed therapy and are ready for termination, I'll write out a certificate for you stating that you've completed so many years of therapy and that you are, in my view, mentally sound."

"Great," the patient enthusiastically replied.

Over the years of his therapy, the patient repeatedly asked the therapist if he thought the patient was ready to terminate. The therapist repeatedly answered no. The patient asked why. The therapist told him: He needed to work through his phobias; he needed to work through his transference; he needed to ana-

252

lyze his resistance; he needed to work through his oral rage; he had not separated from his mother; he had not made peace with his father. In short, the therapist used the patient's desire for a reward (the certificate) as a means to entice him ever more deeply into the therapy process. Ironically, by the time the patient had reached the point where he was ready for termination, he no longer asked the therapist if he was ready.

"Well, I think it's time to start talking about termination," the therapist said one day, suddenly bringing the matter up.

"Really?" The patient seemed almost as anxious as he had been on the first day of treatment. "But what about the problems I'm still having with my father?"

"You said you'd overcome them."

"But they might come back."

"They might."

"And occasionally I still feel angry at my mother."

"You probably always will feel a little angry at her. Analysis can't erase everything."

"So you really think it's time."

"Yes, I think it's time."

"It seems so sudden."

They spent another few months working out the patient's pretermination jitters. When the day arrived for the patient to leave therapy, the therapist brought up the certificate.

"Do you still want it?"

"Nah," the patient replied. "That was just an excuse for avoiding. The contentment and confidence I feel now—those are the rewards of therapy. They're worth much more than any piece of paper."

Intervention 91

The Patient Who Needed More Therapy

A certain female patient and a certain female therapist agreed that the patient was ready for termination. By outward appearances the patient seemed ready. The symptoms that had brought her to therapy had long ago disappeared, and the therapist and patient had maintained a positive and cooperative relationship since then. However, the therapist and patient had unconsciously formed a collusion. The therapist had a need for the patient to be independent, and the patient, needing the therapist's approval, appeared to be ready for independence. All went smoothly until after the termination date. A week later the patient began to regress; her agoraphobia returned and she found herself once again prone to headaches and severe menstrual cramps. It took several weeks for her to call the therapist, because she feared the therapist would disapprove of her relapse and view her as weak and undeserving of the therapist's attention. The therapist discussed the case with her supervisor and understood that her countertransference needs had driven her to push the patient toward termination too soon.

"It's my fault," the therapist told the patient upon her return. "I had a need for you to be independent, and I wasn't paying attention to what was really going on between us. I wanted to hear that you were getting better, and since you needed my approval, you complied."

"I think you're right," the patient said with relief.

"From now on I'd like to hear more about your negative thoughts and feelings."

The patient's cure had been a transference cure, not a real one. Now, for the first time, the patient began expressing her long-avoided negative thoughts and feelings about the therapist and other aspects of her life, and the therapy proceeded for another year, ending successfully. The therapist's intervention—taking responsibility for her error without being self-effacing or seeking the patient's forgiveness or approval—was precisely the adaptation necessary to get the patient on the right track. It immediately alleviated the patient's fears of the therapist's disapproval, gave her permission to express her negative thoughts and feelings, and marked the beginning of the real relationship (as distinguished from the transference relationship).

Intervention 92

The Therapist Who Became His Patient's Pal

Sometimes it happens that a therapist and a patient will have so much in common that a real friendship will form. This therapist and patient were both around the same age and had similar talents, tastes, and interests. In addition, they had both come from similar backgrounds. Both were the favorites of their mothers, and both had fathers who were in some way distant and menacing. Both also had brothers and no sisters and had been raised as Protestants but were no longer religious. Both had become involved in the theater—the therapist as a playwright, the patient as a director. (The former had become a therapist as a second career, when he was in his mid-thirties.) These commonalities made them a good therapeutic match; from the beginning the patient felt deeply understood by the therapist, who had already in his own therapy worked through so many similar issues. A strong therapeutic alliance was maintained throughout the therapy and progress was fairly swift.

During the beginning and middle phases, the therapist had to constantly restrain his friendly impulses toward the patient. The patient might be talking about the theater or one of the other interests they shared in common, and the therapist would want to join in; but he would hold back, knowing that the patient needed a therapist, not a friend, at this point in his development. Their being too friendly might have made it more difficult for the patient to express negative feelings to the therapist; in addition, it would have been using the patient for the therapist's gratification. On some level, the patient would have resented it. However, as the termination phase became imminent, the therapist began to feel a strong kinship with the patient. Indeed, at times he felt he had more in common with this patient than with any of his male friends.

"I'm going to miss our talks," the patient said to him one day. "I have a lot of strong feelings about you. Yes, I admire, respect, and love you, and I think you feel the same way about me."

"You're right. I do feel the same way about you," the therapist replied. "I have a lot of admiration, respect, and love for you, too."

They smiled at each other.

"I sometimes have feelings of regret that you're my therapist, because under different circumstances I think we might have been best friends."

"I've had the same regrets," the therapist admitted.

"Really? Why didn't you tell me this before?"

"You weren't ready to hear it."

"Probably not."

The patient fell silent. In their five years of therapy, they had analyzed everything about their relationship, including their homosexual impulses, their transferences and countertransferences, and their resistances and counterresistances. They were now at peace with each other. At the therapist's request, the patient had begun to sit up during therapy, and he now sat gazing off with a thoughtful glint in his sensitive brown eyes. From the sitting room came the sound of an orchestral piece playing on the radio. He moved his head slightly to the rhythm of the music.

"Copland?" the therapist asked.

"*Rodeo.*"

"Did you ever see the City Ballet's version?"

"It's one of my favorites."

"Mine too."

The therapist, who also had a glint in his brown eyes, began tapping his right foot. The two of them seemed to slide into a reverie, listening to the music in the quiet of the winter afternoon, enjoying this moment of comfort and camaraderie.

"You know," the patient said after a while, "I think maybe we *ought* to be friends after I terminate therapy. Damn it, we really should!"

"Yes, I think so. But we should take a leave of absence from each other to make sure there are no loose ends, therapeutically."

"Right. *You* might find out you still need *me*."

"Right." The therapist chuckled. "One other thing. I must warn you I play a mean game of tennis, and you'll have to endure losing a lot of games."

"I can endure that if you can endure losing to me in chess."

"Absolutely."

The therapist and patient terminated therapy a few months later and then took a one-year leave of absence. Shortly after the year was up the patient called the therapist to ask if he was interested in a game of tennis. They began meeting occasionally for tennis, chess, and other activities. The therapist compiled a 30-10 win-loss record in tennis during the first year of their friendship; the patient compiled a 27-17 win-loss record in chess. They had many intense conversations about the theater, music, women, and relationships—not exactly in that order—and lived amicably thereafter.

Intervention 93

The Patient Who Wanted to Terminate Early

"I've decided to stop," the patient said one day after he had been in therapy for several years. "I feel as if my life is going pretty well now and I've worked out most of the things I came to you for. So I've given it a lot of thought and I've decided to stop at the end of this month." The patient lay silently on the couch.

"Are you waiting for me to say something?" his female therapist asked, as countertransference anxiety pulled at her stomach.

"I suppose I am."

"What would you like me to say?"

"I suppose I'd like you to agree that I'm ready to terminate and I've made the right decision."

"And if I don't agree?"

"Then I'll stop anyway."

"So I have no choice."

"I guess not." The patient sighed, letting out his breath rather loudly. "Well, what's your opinion?" he asked in a tone of irritation.

"I'd like to have the opportunity to explore the question. It may be you *are* ready for termination. But I don't think it should be done abruptly. How about if we start discussing termination without setting a termination date just yet?"

"I really wanted to stop at the end of the month."

"What's your hurry?"

"I don't know."

"You see, that's what we need to find out."

"I don't know if I want to find it out."

The patient reluctantly put off the termination date. Upon further analysis he discovered that his desire to terminate was a resistance to feelings that had begun to emerge due to his transference. His analysis up to that point had been superficial, primarily intellectual, and had not really impacted on his emotions. It was the emotional involvement with his female therapist that he had wished to avoid.

Intervention 94

The Practicing Phase

One of the subphases of what Margaret Mahler described as separation–individuation stage is called the "practicing" phase. During this phase a child is first learning to stand and walk. The child holds on to Mother's knee, then pushes her away and takes a few steps, then goes back for a hug or a touch, then pushes her away again to take another few steps.

The termination phase of a young female patient's therapy seemed to be a recreation of this practicing phase. At a certain point in the therapy process—a point at which she had not completely worked through all her infantile material—the patient decided she needed to leave therapy for a while. "I feel I need to see what it's like to be without you," the patient told her female therapist. At first the therapist had an impulse to hold on to her. Then she realized that this impulse was primarily the result of a concordant identification; she was identifying with the transferred object—the patient's mother. Apparently during the practicing phase this patient's mother had held on to the child, not allowing the child to push her away and "practice" being independent, so that a fixation had developed. When the therapist became aware of her countertransference, she quickly agreed to the patient's request for a leave of absence.

Thus the termination phase for this patient consisted of several years of pushing the therapist away and then returning for the motherly acceptance her own mother had not given her. After the patient had repeated this pattern several times, she was ready to analyze it and to complete the process of termination.

Intervention 95

The Therapist Who Became Overinvolved

She was a beautiful redhead who had been sexually abused by her mother and physically abused by her father and older brothers, a modern Cinderella who radiated vulnerability, sexuality, and innocence. He was a young therapist whose deepest urge as he was growing up in an alcoholic household was to rescue his mother from his abusive father. From the beginning the patient's stories of her childhood abuse touched him, her vulnerability drew him out of himself, and her rather direct sexual innuendoes excited him. He found himself thinking about her all the time, obsessing about her traumatic childhood (wanting to go back and somehow make it right), hatching plans for her rescue from her present lover, who was also abusive, entertaining notions of marrying her and living happily ever after with her. One day, after working with her for about six months, he realized his countertransference had gone too far. All along she had courted him—brought him flowers, declared her love for him, coyly acknowledged her sexual feelings—stirring the fires within him. On this day she had again brought flowers—roses—and then had spent the session crying about a memory of her mother jamming the neck of a bottle up her vagina and saying, "This is what men do to you." At the end of the session she stood and took a shy step toward the therapist, who had also stood up.

"Could I . . . have a hug?"

"Of course!"

He took her into his arms and felt her breath and warmth against his body, and then he found himself kissing her neck and then her cheek and then – her lips. They drew apart, she beaming, he looking rather shocked.

"That was nice," she said.

"I'll see you Monday," he said.

The next day he made a special visit to his supervisor. It did not take long for him to understand what he had to do. Due to his inexperience and to the intensity of the countertransference she had aroused, he had gotten out of control and had endangered the therapy in an irrevocable way. The next time he saw her he apologized for the kiss and explained to her that he was overinvolved and that he would have to terminate therapy with her and refer her to somebody else.

"You mean we have to stop seeing each other completely?"

"That's right."

She sat gaping at him sadly and incredulously. "I don't understand. Why can't I see another therapist and still see you as a friend? I love you. I've never met a man as wonderful as you. Why can't we do that?"

"Because it's not a real relationship. We'd both just be acting out transference feelings. You'd be acting out your need for a good Daddy to rescue you from your mother. I'd be acting out my rescue fantasies about my mother. But after we finished these fantasies, we'd be left with the reality of our present situation."

"And just what is our present situation?"

"In essence we're two lost souls."

"What does that mean?"

"We're two people who lost control and don't really know each other or what the consequences of our actions will be."

"I don't feel out of control," she protested.

He spent several weeks explaining it to her. He went over and over the reasons why they could not see each other anymore, why enacting transference feelings with him would detract from her therapy with her next therapist, how it might damage her personally by creating false hopes. In the end she made a grudging peace with the situation. She went to see her next therapist – a more experienced man – carrying with her the feelings of abandonment, betrayal, and anger from the experience with the first therapist. These feelings propelled her into the new therapy and provided her with the motivation to understand what had happened.

Intervention 96

The Flight to Health

She had been in therapy for a year when she announced to her therapist that she was fine. "What can I tell you? I feel great. I don't have anything to talk about anymore. You've cured me." The next week she announced she would be leaving for an extended trip through Europe. "A friend of mine who works for an airline is getting us free tickets to London, and she also has a friend who invited us to stay at his chateau in the south of France." The therapist could not say anything to her at this time, for he sensed she was not open to feedback. She had gone into a "flight to health" in reaction to the anger and sadness that had begun to surface during the course of her therapy. He did not hear from her for several months, so he decided to telephone her.

"How are you?" he asked.

"I'm still great," she said in a voice that seemed to be straining to be cheerful. "I'm moving to Chicago."

"I thought you were planning to return to therapy after your trip."

"I know, but I've been feeling so great, I didn't think it was necessary."

"How about coming down for a session to discuss it?"

"I can't. I'm leaving tomorrow."

"Then how about calling me when you get to Chicago?"

"Calling you? Why?"

"I've had some thoughts about you since I last saw you, that I'd like to share with you. It's important for your therapy."

"All right," she said with uncertainty. "If you think it's important."

She called him from Chicago at an appointed time, and he told her she had been running away from her feelings and that if she continued to do so it would be destructive for her. He explained the many ways it would be destructive – to her career, to her personal relations, and, of course, to her therapy. "I can understand your desire to terminate therapy," he said, "but I think we should extend the termination process a bit so that you can work through these feelings you're running away from." By the end of the conversation she had become deflated and he had convinced her to continue their therapy on the telephone, once a week, at 7:00 P.M. They did so and she eventually moved back to New York and kept seeing the therapist for another two years; all their sessions during this time were spent discussing, among other things, the pros and cons of termination.

Intervention 97

Termination of a Multiple Personality Patient

Just when the therapist thought he was finished, it happened. For fourteen years he had worked with her. For fourteen years he had hypnotized her, analyzed her, and listened to her cries of deep pain. He had integrated her ten personalities—Jane, Beth, Sue, Robin, Jim, Jack, Mary Beth, Monica, Becky, and Victoria. He had taken her from the first stages of integration, in which her core personality achieved co-consciousness with her alter personalities but all remained separate entities, to the final stages of integration, in which the separate personalities dissolved into one. And then, just as they were speaking of termination, a new personality emerged.

"Hello. I'm Ann."

"Ann?"

"Yes, Ann." She walked into the room and sat down, smiling.

"Oh, no," the therapist said, scratching his ear, perhaps to check whether or not he was hearing things.

"Is something wrong?" she asked him.

"I think Jane's not quite ready to leave therapy."

The patient had spawned another personality as a reaction to the anxiety of termination. However, this new personality was not completely separate from the core personality, and it did not take long to integrate her. Within a few weeks the therapist managed to explore the feelings that had led the patient to regress, and termination moved on without further complications. In this case he did not have to resort to formal hypnosis; the patient had by now been conditioned to perform integration herself. He merely suggested to her that this new personality was yet another aspect of the patient's personality—another unconscious aspect—to be incorporated into her self. "I'd like you to accept Ann just as you've accepted all your other personalities," he told her. "Ann is your unconscious anxiety about separation. Accept her and let's deal with your anxiety."

They did.

Intervention 98

The Therapist and the Recovered Alcoholic

He had been sober for fourteen years. For ten of those years he had been in therapy with a female therapist who was also a former alcoholic. However, on the evening of their last scheduled session, the patient came in drunk.

"So, you're kicking me out, are you?" he said belligerently. The smell of liquor permeated the room. "That's fine with me. I always knew you really couldn't stand me anyway."

"How much did you drink?" the therapist asked matter-of-factly.

"Fuck you."

"All right. I think maybe you'd better leave."

"That's fine with me." The patient stood up, wobbling.

"And I don't want you to call me again until you're sober. When you're completely sober call me and we'll set up another appointment."

"Whatever you say, Doc. You're the boss, Doc."

The patient slammed the door on his way out. The therapist's intervention—asking the patient to leave—served as a negative reinforcement, and her suggestion that he call her when he was sober (making herself available to him at that time) was a positive reinforcement. These were the same kinds of interventions she had used in the beginning phase of treatment, when there had likewise been lapses of alcoholism. These interventions had worked then, and they worked now. The following week he called to make another appointment.

"It seems you've been holding back some feelings," she told him when he returned.

"I guess I do feel kind of like you're kicking me out," he admitted. They spoke about that and other unresolved issues for the next few months, at which time a successful termination took place.

Intervention 99

The Transvestite Who Regressed

He was a transvestite who, during the beginning phase and some of the middle phase, tried to persuade the therapist, an attractive female therapist, to "cross-dress" with him. A married man, he liked to take his wife to "cross-dress" parties, where men and women undressed and put on each other's clothes. He could not understand why the therapist would not agree to cross-dress with him. It seemed like such a harmless request. However, the therapist steadfastly refused, and when his negative transference had become full blown, the patient castigated her for being straight, for being "genderphobic," for being old-fashioned, and other things. She countered by confronting his castration fear.

"Don't you want me to be a woman?" she asked pointedly. She knew that underlying his desire to cross-dress was a need to assuage his castration fear by denying his masculinity (his penis) and viewing her as a phallic woman, all of which harkened back to his narcissistic fixations in early infancy.

As the middle phase wore down and he worked through his anger at the therapist and then at his mother and uncle (he had no father), he developed a more genuine relationship with the therapist and with his wife. More and more, he was able to accept his masculinity and let go of the transvestitism. Then the therapist suggested termination.

"I'm not going to terminate unless you cross-dress with me," the patient said, grinning.

"I thought you were over that?" the therapist said.

"I was. I mean, I haven't cross-dressed in a year. But I'd just like to do it with you, once, before we finish."

"Ah."

"Ah?" The patient looked at the therapist. "Ah?"

"I guess we won't be terminating yet. It seems you still have some erotic feelings to tell me about."

The threat of termination had brought about a regression to transvestitism. The therapist understood immediately that the erotic transference had not been completely resolved, and she intervened by inquiring about the patient's feelings about her and offering appropriate interpretations. After a few months they agreed on a termination date.

Intervention 100

A Sweet and Sorrowful Parting

She was a happily married woman, he a happily married man. Together they plumbed the depths of her psyche, analyzing her through her career conflicts, working her through the feelings left over from her past—the narcissistic mother who had made of her daughter an extension of herself, the abandoning father always off on business trips, the jealous, guilt-inducing little sister. Because of their love for each other, which had developed quickly and held over time, she cooperated with him fully, and things moved on. After a year and a half she was ready for termination. But neither wanted to terminate.

"I love you so much," she told him one day. "I love you with the loneliness and need of a child, yet also with the passion and intellect of a woman."

"I love you too," he said. "I haven't often felt such a rapport, such personal gratification in working with a patient. In fact, I haven't felt this way about anybody, friend or patient."

"I hate for it to have to end."

"I hate it too."

The two sat smiling ruefully at each other.

"Do you think a friendship would work, after termination?"

"What do you think? How would you envision it?"

"Oh, I don't know. I suppose I'd have you and your wife over for dinner. We'd play cards afterwards. Or Scrabble."

"How would your husband feel about having your former therapist over?"

"Well, he has been a little jealous about our relationship. And, now that I think about it, he might feel funny knowing that you know so much about his wife—perhaps more than he does."

"He might."

"And it might be difficult for me not to confide in you. Tell you all the little things that are on my mind."

"Yes."

"I'd want to pull you off somewhere and be alone with you."

"Yes."

"Perhaps it wouldn't work."

"Perhaps not."

"I'm going to miss you."

"I'll miss you too."

By having her envision dining with him and his wife, he helped her to see for herself the problems that might result. Having seen it, she began to resign herself to their eventual parting.

Now and then, when a therapist and patient are very compatible with each other, a real, loving, meaningful relationship can develop, one that transcends the transference relationship. In this instance, the patient had gotten to know the therapist in a real way, particularly toward the end. Indeed, he would sometimes tell her about little irritations he had, and about his wife, his children, his career. This not only helped her in terms of reality testing—letting her know that he too was human—but also allowed the real relationship to unfold. And because of their compatibility, their capacity to trust each other and respect each other's feelings, that relationship had become deeply gratifying to both.

It was also because of their love and respect for each other—

and their love and respect for their spouses—that they were able to restrain themselves from actualizing their relationship outside the therapy office. When they said their good-bye, it was tearless—everything having been already said and felt in previous sessions.

"You'll always be with me," she told him. "Once you have really loved somebody, that love stays with you as a warm reminder of your inner beauty for as long as you live."

Intervention 101

101 Successful Interventions
to Termination

In the beginning the therapist, who was an experienced older man, had to do a great deal of (1) instructing, (2) explaining, and (3) listening. The young woman patient had never been in therapy before; she was highly narcissistic and was frightened of therapy and of her therapist. There were many silences on her part, and he had to counter her silences by (4) asking questions such as "What are you thinking?" or by (5) remaining silent, or by (6) keeping perfectly still, or by (7) generally mirroring her behavior. Several times during the first two years she began to act out treatment-destructive resistances—coming late, canceling appointments, and forgetting to pay her fee. At these times the therapist used (8) confrontation, (9) lecturing, and (10) more instructing and (11) more explaining. Typically, she responded to these interventions by coming on time, paying her fee, and attending all sessions, while remaining silent for long periods of time in order to spite the therapist–father. He would again counter with (12) silence and (13) mirroring. At other times she spoke of wanting to move to the country or of not being able to afford therapy. The therapist would usually react by (14) questioning her about her reasons for wanting to move, or just

(15) listening and (16) making noises to show he was listening. Once, when the patient announced she might have to quit therapy in a month because she didn't have the money, he (17) mirrored her behavior and countered her threat by (18) giving her an ultimatum: "If you don't get the money for therapy I may have to drop you." On another occasion she failed to appear for a session and he (19) telephoned her, (20) questioned her about her motives, and (21) suggested she come in for a session later that day. When she appeared, he at first countered her silence by (22) remaining silent. Then (23) he told her a story about a girl who had held her breath until she was blue and exploded into a million pieces. Then (24) he expressed his annoyance at her obstinate silence and (25) gave her a lecture about how she was sabotaging her therapy. This succeeded in bringing out her transference rage, which she expressed for the remainder of the hour, primarily by putting down both him and the therapy. He (26) listened to her tirade, (27) said, "Ouch!" when she said something cutting, then (28) complimented her at the end of the session for expressing her feelings instead of running away. As she left he (29) smiled more brightly than usual and (30) explained that this session was a turning point.

In the middle phase the patient got stuck in a negative transference for more than a year. Gradually the therapist helped her to work through and analyze her angry feelings and critical thoughts by (31) having her lie on the couch, (32) suggesting that she attend more frequently, (33) mirroring her negativity with his own, (34) joining her resistance by saying, "Maybe I *am* inadequate as a therapist," and the like, (35) telling stories, (36) countering her sarcasm with his own, (37) challenging her resistance by saying, "If you want to hold on to your anger, go ahead and see what happens!", (38) identifying with the patient when she complained he did not understand her by relating an incident in which he had experienced similar feelings, (39) giving her a homework assignment to draw a picture of her father, and (40) continually interpreting her father, brother, and mother transferences. In the middle of the fourth year she developed an intense erotic transference. For the next year she urgently professed her love for the therapist, unleashing her repressed yearning for merger with Mother and her oedipal desires for Father. The therapist (41) listened to her utterances with an attitude of acceptance and (42) now and then said, "Those are good feelings." He sometimes (43) interpreted that she was getting in touch with infantile feelings and memories, some from preverbal times. "It's not really me you long for with such intensity, but your mother," he would say. Often she cried for long periods of time. The therapist would (44) remain silent and (45) be still for the most part, sometimes (46) making statements of identification with her sorrow ("I know how you feel"). Then for a period of months she insisted she wanted to sleep with the therapist. She had never known a man like him, so kind, so brilliant, so loving, and she just wanted to make love to him once, just once. She became stuck in this place, and the therapist tried many interventions to advance the therapy. He tried (47) making further interpretations about the genetic antecedents of her present feelings; (48) questioning her about her sexual fantasies about him; (49) explaining the reality of the situation (it would be harmful and unethical); (50) telling her stories; (51) letting her go on for sessions without his saying anything; (52) expressing irritation at being constantly badgered about having sex with her; (53) making statements showing identification and empathy for her pain; (54) mirroring her; and (55) making paradoxical statements ("Maybe we ought to do it and throw caution to the wind"). This last intervention finally succeeded in getting her to let go of her demand to sleep with him, allowing her to analyze her need to do this. The therapist (56) offered various interpretations having to do with narcissistic and oedipal fixations. During the fifth year of therapy they continued to analyze her transference and resistance. By this time the therapist was using mainly interpretations. He interpreted (57) her transferences to him, (58) her relationships with men, (59) her career conflicts, and

(60) her relationship with her parents. When she went back to college after having dropped out for six years, he (61) complimented her and helped her decide, by (62) questioning her, on a fitting major. He also (63) made suggestions as to which elective courses would be most suitable. When her mother died, he (64) consoled her, (65) remained silent while she cried, (66) made a statement of identification by relating how he had felt when his mother had died, and (67) questioned her about other feelings. She acknowledged, after a few sessions, the anger she felt at her mother for dying, and the therapist (68) listened and (69) explained that it was all right to have that anger. At times he (70) exhorted her to "get it off your chest." After they had worked through her anger, she got in touch with her existential issues — her resentment about her own mortality, her need to find a meaning in a world that seemed, particularly now, to be "a tale told by an idiot." The therapist (71) sympathized with her and (72) revealed his own resentment about death. She asked how he had handled his resentment, and he (73) explained how he had made peace with death and with an apparently senseless world by laying stress on closeness with the primary figures in his life. Soon after, the patient met a man with whom she fell in love, and she spent many sessions discussing the feelings this new relationship brought up. The therapist interpreted (74) her feelings of inadequacy, (75) of penis envy, (76) of separation anxiety from her mother, and (77) of the fear of dependency. He had already made these interpretations many times before, but now they seemed to hit home. He (78) told stories about other women who had gotten married, (79) made suggestions about how she might better cope with her anxiety, and (80) supported her ego: "You're strong enough now to handle this." After the marriage and honeymoon, the patient went through a period of adjustment with her husband, and these conflicts were discussed with the therapist. He (81) listened, (82) questioned her, and (83) made interpretations relevant to the situation. More and more his relationship with the

patient had become a real one, and he (84) acknowledged conflicts he had had in his own marriage and (85) explained how he had solved them.

In the termination phase the therapist began to relate to her as he would to a friend: (86) being honest with her about any feelings she aroused in him, (87) discussing common interests, (88) providing her with practical information (about becoming a therapist herself), and sometimes even (89) asking her advice. However, when it came time to actually set a date for termination, the patient was hesitant. The therapist (90) insisted it was time, but told her (91) the termination date could be extended if she needed more time. That seemed to help her accept termination for a while. Then she sank into a depression that was almost as deep as the one she had been in when she first entered therapy. The therapist intervened with (92) silence and (93) questions about what she was feeling. Having become familiar with her feelings by now, she could tell him she was feeling abandoned by him. He interpreted that this was rekindling (94) her infantile feelings of having been left by her mother in a nursery school at age 3, and also (95) the rejection she had experienced by her distant, alcoholic father. The therapist (96) explained the reality of the situation—that he was not abandoning her, that rather he was giving her the final push toward independence and growth; and he (97) acknowledged that it was hard for him to let her go. She said she had grown to love him and would always love him. He (98) said he loved her, too, and would remember her lovingly. By the time her final session arrived, she was excited about life without therapy. She asked the therapist for a good-bye hug, which (99) he gave her. She asked again if she could call him if she needed him, and he again (100) reassured her that she could. As she left (101) he called after her to wish her good luck.